APPLES & ORANGES

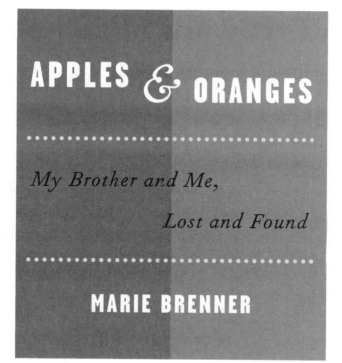

APPLES & ORANGES

My Brother and Me, Lost and Found

MARIE BRENNER

SARAH CRICHTON BOOKS

Farrar, Straus and Giroux • New York

Sarah Crichton Books
Farrar, Straus and Giroux
18 West 18th Street, New York 10011

Distributed in Canada by Douglas & McIntyre Ltd.
Printed in the United States of America
First edition, 2008

Library of Congress Cataloging-in-Publication Data
Brenner, Marie.
    Apples and oranges : my brother and me, lost and found / Marie Brenner.—
1st ed.
        p.   cm.
    "Sarah Crichton books."
    ISBN-13: 978-0-374-17352-4 (alk. paper)
    ISBN-10: 0-374-17352-4 (alk. paper)
    1. Brenner, Marie—Family.   2. Novelists, American—21st century—
Biography   3. Cancer.   I. Title.   II. Title: Apples and oranges.

PS3552.R384Z465   2008
813'.54—dc22
[B]

                                                                    2008008929

Designed by Abby Kagan
Endpaper photograph by James Pomerantz

www.fsgbooks.com

10 9 8 7 6 5 4 3 2 1

For Casey, Ernie, and my brother Carl

Our very eyes are sometimes like our judgments, blind.

—*Cymbeline*

Every memoir is filtered through the gauze of a writer's memory. Wherever possible, I have referred to letters, diaries, and research to amplify my ability to recall and imagine my family, present and past. I have also changed the names of some of the people mentioned in this book and disguised aspects of their lives. Conversations, events, and dialogue have been reconstructed as well. This is very much my own version of my life.

PREFACE

· ·

Every life has moments that change us forever and make us who we are. I heard that line recently in a movie trailer and wrote it down in the dark of the City Cinemas on East Eighty-sixth Street in New York City. I cannot tell you what movie the trailer was advertising, but I knew as soon as I heard the voice-over that, however hokey, the line was absolutely true.

This is a book about a brother and a sister coming together in midlife. I started writing it as an investigation into siblings, searching for an alternate universe in which I could explore my own family.

Okay, more to the point, my brother and me.

And then, of course, there were the apples. Always, apples.

There is one more thing: I could never have written this book if my brother were still alive. This is my story and the story of my brother as we struggled to find a way to be in each other's life. For years we failed at that. And so much else. Neither of us knew why that was the way it was. We just knew we had to try to make it better.

It took us a very long time.

Sometimes you do not get to understand everything.

APPLES *&* ORANGES

1

We fight at the dinner table.

Stay away from my apple farms, my brother Carl says.

And stay away from the Cascades.

You don't know anything about apples.

It is a tone that I know well. The mixture of hate and love, rage and need, all scrambled together.

It is not easy for him to breathe. His girlfriend, Frika, is by his side, acting as if everything is as it always has been, as if nothing in the world is the matter. She is oh-so-British, drops her voice at the end of questions, takes on like the queen. She pulls me aside in the kitchen and says, "He is the love of my life and always has been. We have never been happier." Her cheeks flush like a debutante's.

Her black lace nightgown hangs on a hook in his bathroom. At night, they stay up late and listen to *Parsifal,* Wagner's dark score of the holy fool. Her eyes gleam with pools of longing. She looks at him as if he is Devonshire cream. At the dinner table, she hums a few stanzas from *Das Rheingold.* "Fricka's theme!" she says. Her expression says it: *Top that.*

He eats two helpings of filet, then asks for a second dessert.

Tarte tatin.

Made by the other girlfriend, who was at his house for lunch.

"Heather sure knows how to cook," he says.

A shadow passes over Frika's face.

At lunch, Heather demonstrated her pastry-cutting technique. "I always put a crimped leaf on the top for Carl," she said.

"He is the love of my life," she said.

There are always apples around him. Women, too. Apple pie. Big, chic antique bowls of wooden apples in all colors: red and gold and striped. Apple ceramics, apple pencils, apple photos. Produce labels framed on the library wall: Gulf Brand Texas Vegetables from the Rio Grande Valley, Empire Builder, Wenatchee District Red Seal Brand. I am an American first, then a Texan, he would say, not understanding he sounded like Augie March. The clues are there, in the grad school classic *Augie March*, I later realize. "A man's character is his fate," Saul Bellow wrote, quoting Heraclitus.

You always have to show off and tell us what you know, Carl said.

"I'll be in Washington next week," I say. "I have an interview. I have to close a piece."

"You promised me," he says. "You said you would stay away from Washington State. You sat right here and said that you would not go to the Cascades."

He yells as loudly as I have ever heard him.

"Washington, D.C.," I shout back.

I have the trait as well.

He glares. I glare. In that glare is the jolt of our connection, the fierceness of our attachment. We stare at each other hard.

"I don't know what you are so angry about," he says.

The next morning, he is at his desk when I say good-bye. It's a bright Texas morning. March 29, 2003. The *San Antonio Express-News* had a headline the day before: "Deployment. Fort Hood's 4th Infantry Division Moves Out." The country is now at war and we are in San Antonio, a city of military bases. Starbucks on Broadway is filled with young army officers from Fort Sam Houston. They wear camouflage clothes and are on their way to Baghdad. "Macchiato skim," one says.

Fort Sam Houston, the country club of the army, borders the lush suburb of Alamo Heights. It's an oasis of privilege with a Texas zip code that is used conversationally—"09," for 78209, the demographic of debutantes and ranch kings, fiesta princesses, new-money Latinos and WASP bankers with Roman numerals after their names, some of which date back to the Battle of the Alamo.

"What do you think of the war?" I ask a woman I went to high school with. "I don't watch anything depressing," she says. "I know y'all are concerned about 9/11, but we feel so safe down here."

Starbucks had a swarm of kids leaving for Iraq, I say when I walk up the stairs of Carl's house. He has a shredder next to him, and at the moment I arrive, he is filling it with orchard reports, glossy brochures for Procure Fertilizers, invitations for dinners at the McNay Art Museum. I think nothing of this. He is a neat freak who shreds everything that crosses his desk. He has always lined up his pencils and sharpened them just so.

On the wall where he works is a large map of South Africa in the Boer years, framed in antique gold, and several pictures of our grandfather, Isidor, a man of committees and awards, donating his specimen camellia bushes to a worthy cause. It is a mystery to me why Carl has kept a shrine to a relative he did not know. He looks out of large windows with window seats to neat stone houses of 78209 and bright lawns with a sea of bluebonnets in the grass. You know it's March in Texas when you take to the hill country and see an unending blue mist covering the fields.

Carl's bloodwork is coming through the fax. He stares at the numbers. He is now a student of the CRP test, which measures inflammation and must read 3 or less; the CEA; the glutathione test, which is a barometer of the liver; a new one, the CA 19-9, with its Geiger counter to monitor the pancreas; the prothrombin, which tells you about clotting; the remnant lipo test, IDL plus VLDL3.

My CEA is going nuts, he says.

It is just a number, I reply too quickly. *These numbers go up and down. You know that.*

He's working with an assistant, a woman I have met through someone at the gym. I pretend, just like Frika, that everything is as it always has been. That I can escape. That my brother is normal. That this time in his life is just a challenge, a euphemism I use all the time. That his condition is "chronic." Something to be handled. Another euphemism. I am going back to my home in New York City. Just six hours away, I tell myself. We have blown past whatever went on the night before. We always do. Anger is our Prozac. I am trying to train myself to say: I love it when you're angry! You sound like you did when you were fourteen! Or: Here you go again! That wonderful juicy aliveness! Rage! Instead, I yell back and get stuck in a whirl of fury—what the Buddhists call samsara—the endless repetition of a treadmill, the prison I am in.

You have the best doctors in the country.

I know, he says.

This is manageable, I say.

I love you more than anyone, I say. *You are my brother. We are Brenners. Team Carl.*

There is no epiphany. There are no final words.

"Don't leave me," he says Tears run down his cheeks. "I am sorry for everything."

"I will be back in four days," I say. "Nothing bad is going to happen. There is nothing to worry about."

"No one ever tells you the truth," Carl says.

He fills jumbo lawn-and-leaf Hefty bags with files. "House-cleaning," he says. A copy of the New Testament is on his desk. I see a box marked "Orchard."

"Father Jesus," he now says before every meal, "we pray for our troops in Iraq."

I have a list in the car. Last-minute sources to double-check: Queries from Mary Flynn, the chief of research for the magazine at which I work. Phone calls I must make to Paris in the next twenty-four hours. Phrases to double-check and translate for the text: My notes on a legal pad—"*On piege les mecs*: Is this the idiom for 'one sets a trap'?" A review of a Leonardo da Vinci show of drawings at the Met, from *The New York Review of Books*. I have circled the word "sfumato." Later, I search it on Wikipedia.

Sfumato

"*Sfumato* is the Italian term for a painting technique which overlays translucent layers of colour to create perceptions of depth, volume and form. In particular, it refers to the blending of colours or tones so subtly that there is no perceptible transition."

In Italian, *sfumato* means "vanished," with connotations of "smoky," and is derived from the Italian word *fumo*, meaning "smoke." Leonardo described "sfumato" as "without lines or borders, in the manner of smoke or beyond the focus plane."

I always tell everything I know.

Why are you always interrupting? Carl always says.

I regret everything.

If Carl could speak, what would he say?

2

The word always used for my brother in the family is "perplexing." It's a Southern word, what you say when you don't want to say what you really think, one of those perfect tapioca words that just begin to hint at the mountain underneath.

How perplexing? Take the box of pears that arrives each year. Like everything with Carl, what seems an act of generosity—a huge box of fruit from his orchards in Washington State—comes with a tax, the Carl tax. In this case, the tax was the inevitable series of demanding and annoying phone calls that precede the box's arrival and drain every bit of pleasure from the gift. His voice would be tense on the telephone, with a tone of drop-everything attention, rebuke on the edge of the scenario. He is, he said, in the middle of harvest, in the fields with the Mexican pickers from dawn until dark. "Do you know how busy I am?"

Then: "Are you going to be home between two p.m. and four p.m. on Friday?"

"I don't know."

"You have to be there. The fruit is coming. It must go into the refrigerator immediately."

"Why?" Big mistake.

"It starts to turn. These pears are precious. Do you know how much trouble they are to pick?"

His tone is icy.

The first call would have a follow-up: *Where are you going to put the fruit?* He would wait for the answer—*the refrigerator*—before gliding on to the next command: *Don't give this fruit away. It is special.* Always there is the implication that I will not handle them well. I will be reckless. Somehow the pears will bruise.

Finally the box arrives. The fruit inside is wrapped in white foam sleeves with special holes, pears wearing socks. There are layers of purple and pink padding, plastic sheets called Panta-Paks. The box is embedded in layers of brown tape, as if it were a can of Mace. And inside is the note. "I picked them myself. Don't give them away."

So, what to do with twenty-four Asian pears the size of softballs? They are Arirangs, a variety popular in Chinatown and in Napa restaurants for use in salads with endive and walnuts, raisins or escarole. This Arirang pear arrived in Washington State from Korea as a cutting and was replanted in a greenhouse, then moved to a grove of experimental trees not far from the Canadian border. A nurseryman named Moon grafted the cutting to a rootstock, spending years trying to get it to reproduce in Washington's sandy soil. It was crucial that the flesh of the pear stay as white as a baby's tooth. There could not be a blemish or a pore. It would somehow have to grow at the bottom of a limb—which could be achieved by pruning but required long consultations with the experts at the experimental station at Washington State University, who weighed in on how to prune and clip the leaves so that it could be easier to pick. Because the easier to pick, the less likely the workers were to bruise the fruits as they plucked them from the trees.

Then, there was the matter of the codling moth and the gypsy moth larvae, the Antichrists of orchard life. More experts would come to stand and stare at the tree for hours with tiny instruments that looked like the world's smallest spyglasses. They could study the branches of a tree going this way and that and gaze at limbs that no one outside an orchard could hope to understand. And all of it to pull off a tree a brown, fuzzy pear that could be sold in Japan—but in few other markets—at $20, where it inevitably would be wrapped in a colored cellophane and given out at naming ceremonies at Buddhist temples.

I will learn all of this years after I first arrive in Wenatchee, and it will be but a tiny mosaic of the knowledge that I come to acquire, but none of it from Carl, who hoards his horticulture facts and nurses his grafting methods in secret, as well as his singular ability each year to turn out eleven million Gala and Braeburn apples, Bosc and Anjou pears. The fruit is just one of my brother's mysteries, along with the yearly boxes, the insane fetish over the packing of them, his lack of trust in me or anyone. Put all that in the same category as the neat-freak closets and the shoes polished and hung up in a row. I am convinced—and state loudly to anyone who is near me—that Carl's closet and his multiple obsessions are a sure sign of OCD. All of the records point to it, the notes kept pristinely, the dates he makes that are never changed. The rage at anyone who does.

Could anyone have less in common with a brother? I live in a wind tunnel of paper and sneak Zone bars in the afternoon and worry about the two hundred calories. I have a long history of lost tapes of crucial interviews, once leaving on the D.C.–New York shuttle four hours of tapes with Iran-contra special prosecutor Lawrence Walsh, a sourpuss who spent much of our interview complaining about a former assistant who had gone to glory writing tell-alls about the doings in Walsh's office. I like to imagine someone finding those tapes on the plane and hearing Walsh's accusations spewing forth in that Washington afternoon of 1993. At that moment, I thought Walsh and his opinions mattered, had some importance, could change things.

Have I forgotten to mention the assault that always came after the box of fruit arrived? There would be the following questions:

Were any of the Asians bruised?
Are you sure?
Did you open the box yourself?
What time did it arrive?
Did you keep the slip?
Can I demand a refund from UPS?

3

It started with a letter, as always with Carl, carefully thought out.
I am writing to you to ask you to help me save my life.
That was the headline, what it was really about.
The actual letter, in fact, was this:

Dear Marie:
I have a lot to tell you. I have put this in writing so you can
absorb it quietly. Then let's talk on the phone. You might be able
to save my life. If I limit myself to what the FDA has approved,
I could be dead in three months to a year. With some luck, a drug
in a clinical trial may keep me alive and fully active for some
time. A cure may be discovered in the interim. No one knows.
That is the reality. Marie, I didn't want to break all this to you
when you were on deadline with the sugar article or the day
before Thanksgiving. When we talk on the phone, I'll bring you
up to date on some other measures I have taken.

Until I find this letter again, five years later, I have never
noticed, or did not remember and did not think it was odd, that a

sticker had been pasted covering the second paragraph. I hold it up to the light and can easily read a paragraph my brother wrote, reconsidered, partially reconsidered, did not decide to wipe out on his computer, but instead simply obscured the salient point:

I don't want family, friends, employees, and business associates to "hear" about this matter until I am ready to tell them personally. What I have to communicate is for your eyes only, at this time. It is for me to decide to whom and when to disclose it. When I am ready to disclose it to Casey, Ernie and everyone else in the family, any of my friends or any of your friends, that is for me to decide. I strongly implore you to honor my request 100%.

He wrote it out carefully on a laptop that he had to punch in his special code to get into: Wotan. Wotan was, Wagner buffs know, the king of the gods, father of Brünnhilde and Siegmund, brought to a bad ending in the *Ring* cycle. The last moment is not quick on the uptake, coming seventeen hours of Wagner later, when Valhalla, the home of the gods, goes up in flames.

Every day, that was the code he used: WOTAN.

Casey finds me crying in my bedroom.

"I thought you hated your brother," she says.

Casey, an only child, finds it difficult to understand the underbrush of our connection. She has a book bag on her shoulders, her dark hair is pulled back in a ponytail.

Mom, she says, then sits down hard on the bed. Neither of us speak. There is silence between us, nothing we can say.

Then: "Is Uncle Carl going to die?" she asks quietly. "What are we going to do?"

4

I am late this morning for a parents' meeting scheduled at Casey's school. I am trying to gird myself for the mothers of the senior class. I imagine all of us putting on the armor for the day. I try for a reasonable imitation of appropriateness, pull out a black blazer and gray flannel pants. The mothers have a subtle way of weighing you with their eyes, asking you pointed questions like *Are you still going to that nutritionist?*, pricing your cashmere blazer, looking over your shoulder to see who else is in the room. *If you are falling apart, make sure you have on your best shoes and pearls*, my mother always said.

And why was that, exactly?

Nine-thirty a.m.

Uh-oh.

I can't get out of my pajamas, dazed from the grenade that has been suddenly lobbed into the house. Why did Carl not mention a word when he was here the last four days? There was not the slightest hint that anything was wrong. On Thanksgiving morning, he ran four miles in Central Park, complained about the traffic backup from the parade, then worked his way through triple helpings of stuffing and woefully overcooked turkey, finished the guacamole, and had a trio of desserts, scooping up the last of the plum crisp that my stepson James made. Why did I even open the FedEx when I saw his return address? I assumed it was a Carl communication, some interminable legal document. He's been coping with our father's slow deterioration, and there have been endless letters flying back and forth.

I hear the FedEx drop through my mail slot. Don't open this, I think. It can wait. It's only Carl. What in the world could this be about? Why didn't he bring these papers with him? It wasn't like him to spend $30 to send a FedEx when he was going to be seeing me in New York. *I don't waste money like you do,* he always says.

I have to get to the school. The gray pants are at the cleaner's and now there is a heap of black ones on the bed. I wear the jeans with a turtleneck and repeat out loud: *This is who I am.* Why am I worried about my clothes when my brother isn't going to live? What is wrong with me? What did I miss on Thanksgiving? Our days together were like always with my older brother: me over-scheduling activities like Virginia Woolf's Mrs. Dalloway to keep the silences away. We have a history of stupid arguments, minuscule fissures, black holes. Our relationship is like tangled fishing line. We are defined by each other and against each other, a red state and a blue state, yin and yang. How typical that he would send this news in a letter written in a lawyer's prose. He's always kept his feelings pushed away with a barge pole. I have seen him cry only once, at the age of twenty-one. A boxed set of LPs came into our house. *Parsifal.* It was a gift sent from Mexico City by fun-loving, boozy Aunt Dorothy, who lived with a tenor from the Bellas Artes known for his big-voice Puccini arias. "Charles adores this recording and sends you muchos besos!" Dorothy wrote.

Carl took the records off to his bedroom. The sound filled the house for hours. I banged on the door. It took him a few moments to answer, and when he did, he had tears running down his cheeks. *You are a freak*, I said.

Now, this Monday morning, the telephone rings and it is my friend Jane calling from Washington. We've known each other since our early twenties. "What is the matter?" she says, hearing my voice.

For years, she has heard me bang on about my brother. In the 1970s, when he would come to New York and start a rant about Nixon and the Vietnam War, not understanding why my new friends, "these New York libs," would not see that you could not give Southeast Asia to the Commies. A letter arrived in his college days that telegraphed his thoughts:

> *As to letting the commies have S.E. Asia, why not let them have Mexico? The very thought of giving them another inch of land is ridiculous. My solution is to drop some big firecrackers on their cities and kill them wholesale. The news on the radio here is that we have just retaken our Embassy after the VC captured the first floor. This and the Pueblo incident is excuse for bombing them into oblivion.*

A decade or so later, he was in New York railing against "you people in the media who have ruined the apple business with that fake Alar report." By then, he had set up in the orchards of Washington and was apoplectic when *60 Minutes* ran a junk science exposé about the pesticide Alar, drawing in the actress Meryl Streep to defend the apple juice of American schoolchildren. Such was the hysteria over Alar that was pumped up wrongly by an environmental group that children would stay home from school to not have to eat applesauce in their cafeterias. "You are part of an irresponsible profession of yellow journalists," he said. "And you have destroyed the good people of Washington State."

"Do you know anyone for my brother?" I once asked Jane.

"You mean Carl, who did not come to either of your weddings? You're fixing him up again?" Jane asked.

He was recently divorced and I was trying to help him meet women.

Jane thinks of him the way all my friends do, that he is just there, a fixture at holidays, unknowable, charm-free.

"Carl? Are you kidding?" she asked. "I mean, he's good-looking, but he is a right-wing nut."

Now I am crying on the telephone.

"You have to understand him," I say.

"I do understand," she says. "He's weird."

5

. . . .

NEW YORK CITY
THANKSGIVING, 1999

This year the box of fruit Carl has sent is full of his precious and rarest Jonagolds, which he calls the caviar of fruit. Something I am now ashamed of is that at this late date I had yet to visit his orchards, even though he had owned them for fifteen years. We were on two sides of the country and could put our phone calls to each other on an egg timer. Often when he called I would wave my hand at my husband or daughter and mouth, *Not here.*

His first move upon entering my house is to look in the refrigerator to make sure that the Jonagolds are properly stored. Still in their socks! "Good," he says. "You listened to me. For a change." Later that afternoon, he cautions James to not, under any circumstances, bake them, cook them, or serve them in any way that is not raw. "They are not cooking apples! These Jonagolds are precious! Is that clear?"

James is a photographer, but he is also a tremendous cook, a former pastry chef. I watch him brace himself, reacting to the tone.

"Marie has insisted that she will do all the cooking this year," James says.

"What?" Carl replies.

A few words to explain the situation, the thrum of tension in our house:

Casey is applying to college, early decision. Need I say more? In the last two weeks alone, Casey has threatened to move to her father's and then stood over me when the FedEx man came to take her application, so that I would address the envelope. We are in the nightmare of launch time, the push-pull, love-hate mother-daughter roller coaster of senior year. My husband, Ernie, has an attitude. "It will all be fine," he says. "Wherever she goes." He believes it. But then there are, as Carl calls us, the Women. Or, okay, I admit it: me. I have started putting signs on her bedroom door, the way my mother once did with me, koans to take away because it was clear, Casey told me on a weekly basis, that after she took off for college, that was it! She would be free of me. So: this one, from God knows where, ALL MEN MEAN WELL.

"So Hitler meant well?"

Casey attends one of those high schools where the parents have been getting strafed by teachers and administrators about the college application process since the kids were in middle school, with everyone all the while repeating the mantra: There is no pressure. By that they mean that "no pressure" is the buzz around the halls about the kid who glued his application onto a basketball and sent it off to Brown. At cocktail parties in New York, accomplished women in expensive dresses vibrate with what it means to have an eleventh grader hovering on the brink of "the college thing." A rule I have always tried to live by is never, ever go to a parents' meeting; nothing but trouble awaits you there. But this year, I have lost my center and seem to be at school all the time.

"All I want is for Casey, once in her life, to have seen her mother prepare an entire Thanksgiving meal from scratch," I say.

Now I am on the floor in the middle of the kitchen. I don't know how to puree parsnips. "How can you not know how to puree parsnips?" Ernie says. He's a cook too, like James. "There's a logic to it," he says. "You parboil them and then you run them through the Cuisinart with a little cream and a touch of ginger—maybe some cardamom. Why is this so hard? You don't need a recipe for something so easy. Who would ever use a recipe for anything?"

I have tried to ban him from the kitchen because I don't want to hear the remarks about the ceramic knife that will chop everything faster and I don't want to hear that I am ruining his $100 sushi knife by using it to chop celery.

"Honey," my friend Peggy says when she sees me down on the floor, "we don't have to be cooks. We can put meals together that are reasonable. We don't have to be everything to everybody."

As it happens, I am also on deadline, at the beginning of trying to understand a complicated case that will drag on for months and involve two crusading public interest lawyers who have decided to take on Big Sugar amid allegations that thousands of Jamaican cane cutters have been cheated by some of the richest and most powerful Cuban Americans on the planet.

"What kind of message," I ask, "does it send Casey that there are eleven restaurants on speed dial in this house?"

At the table, Carl is distracted. He stares out at the garden, then helps himself to seconds and thirds of pumpkin pie.

"Uncle Carl, did you know that my mother woke me up at three in the morning and asked me if I thought I had enough safety schools?" Casey says.

"I did not," I say. "That's absurd. It was more like ten o'clock. And I had just come from a parents' meeting. They made me nuts."

"That sounds like your mother," my brother says. "She's kind of crazy."

"Tell me about it," Casey replies. "I hope I am spared the gene pool."

"I can't believe you think that cooking is so hard," Carl says. "Why is everything always bought prepared? You waste so much damn money. You could learn to cook again if you wanted to. You weren't so bad a cook in college. I liked your chicken Parmesan when you didn't overcook it."

Years ago, we went to the same colleges—three years apart—crossing at Penn and later at the University of Texas when Carl was in law school and I was a transfer student getting an undergraduate degree.

I am trying to explain how complicated my life has been with my brother. "You sure spend a lot of time together for two people who don't have much in common," Peggy says.

Much later, I will find the photograph at the bottom of the box marked "Orchard" that he kept near his desk. It was a time in his life when he had retreated more or less to a motel in Washington's Cascade Mountains, preferring a one-room container to the clamor of a city, to the necessity of absorbing the opinions of other people.

6

Carl in his orchard, posed over a faded red wooden bin of glowing, shining fruit. It is impossible to tell if the bin held his Braeburns, Jonagolds, or Galas. He was unusual-looking; handsome, many thought. He had strong, chiseled features, a Roman nose, a wide brow, and Slavic cheekbones that many in our family share. In the picture, he holds Callie, his sheepdog-mutt combination, discovered abandoned on a Texas highway. A city-born boy, Carl looks directly into the camera with a smile I have rarely seen. His happiness has come from fruit, from Anjou and Bosc pears, from Goldens and Braeburns and Red Fujis. There are apples and more apples, a tub of reds gleaming in the sun, each apple as exquisite as a Vermeer.

The orchard covers a hillside. His hillside, his orchards, his land. Behind him is a sky, a dome of blue, the mountains of Washington a parfait of golds and reds. Most of the apples of the United States are grown here, then stamped with the cheery little red apple sticker that says WASHINGTON STATE. It is a region of mountains dotted with fruit trees, an American pastoral spread over many miles with towns whose names sound like Indian tribes—Yakima, Walla Walla, Wenatchee.

When Carl, at thirty-five, announced he had decided to give up his career as a courtroom lawyer to spend his life learning the secrets of cultivating fruit, he astonished everyone who knew him. "Carl," my father said, "Jews don't farm."

But he has thrown off the shirt of family, given up a career as a trial lawyer, and morphed into Apple Man, which is what we now call him behind his back.

We called him that on Thanksgiving Day.

Apple Man!

"Is that a joke?" he asked.

He was shut down on the subject of his love of fruit, at least then.

Apples? How could he explain that he saw them as a sign of America and its possibilities down the long stream of history, of apple fairs and cider orchards and contests for the best apples of the year. It made him shiver with everything he considered crucial: *America the Beautiful.* He learned not to say that out loud around my friends. He stood at the top of his first orchard and stared toward the Columbia Valley, the river beneath him, the sun glinting off the trees, breaking in shards over the trees, so clear it became one of his many secrets, carried in his heart. He could never find the words to describe even to his own friends that moment when you drive the Cascade Loop and suddenly see the first sign of the green soldiers lined up on the hillsides in neat diagonals, somber against the bright turquoise of the big sky. It sounded so corny, he thought.

Carl could talk your head off about America and how it sold out its farmers, carrying on about America as it was, as it could have been and is not, and if you wound him up, he could move on to what he considered with some cause was the complete scam—his word—of organic farming and the ridiculousness of "food with a face." And this would lead into another tirade about the new trend for community-based farming and the boxes of scrubby kale and wormy peaches that were now delivered to your door. Who were these people, exactly? He believed that anyone who was taken in by "a bunch of ex-hippies looking to regroup" was an idiot. That's what my brother called the mimeo-producing, back-to-nature crowd blogging out there in Vermont and Washington State about the glories of their crops.

He had a phrase he used:

Just Good Fruit.

That's what he wanted America to consume.

That's what he produced.

I study the photograph carefully. He's lean and brown from the sun. He is savoring every moment, the colors of the land, the beauty of what he is growing. My image of my brother is so at odds with this Johnny Appleseed. How did I never know this stranger? I immediately blame him: He hid his personality, keeping this Carl in a closet so that I could never see him. Surely, this was intentional.

A wall divided us. I feel ashamed at my inability to see or appreciate this Carl. Where did I fail at being an acceptable younger sister?

How could I describe the feeling that came over me when my brother and I were together, the sense that the world had become a landscape of no colors? And why did I feel compelled to buoy up this stranger and his emotions of poured cement?

Here we are, Carl and me.

Winter, San Antonio, 1953.

Look at us before we dive into our battle stations, caught by our mother on the front step of our brand-new house. In downtown San Antonio, there is a large sign up at the Majestic Theater: COLORED BALCONY. On Wednesdays, our cafeteria serves local Tex-Mex specialties, tamales and refried beans. Our birthday parties include piñatas, mariachis, and boat rides down the San Antonio River that borders the barrio. Eisenhower is president and our father is angry. *A general! Who would ever turn the country over to someone who came up in the military!* He's angry at everything these days. His older brother, Henry, sits in his office at the store, surrounded by rabbis. "Henry can't make a decision on any subject! Rabbis! This would have never happened in the military!" he says. That's how he sounds all the time, commanding, filled with opinions that often collide. Very Texas, boastful and confident as if he'd been born in a uniform. He's been in the war and talks about it all the time. *You should have smelled Calcutta from the air! My God, India! The Brits called my boys in Calcutta the wogs, those sons of bitches!*

We look out to a forest of cactus and maguey and palomino Thoroughbreds that belong to a neighbor, an air-conditioning king. In the photograph, I am a textbook younger child, pulling focus, training for my role as bête noire to my brother Carl. He's barely six years old and has already developed the Carl Look. It's the expression that the rabbit gets in *Watership Down* when it goes *tharn*, freezes in the light.

Apples and Oranges.

That's what our mother calls us.

She, a beautiful blonde, has left her Boston family for life in San Antonio in what she describes to her mother in letters as "a very unusual and colorful family." That's Thelmaspeak when she doesn't want to tell you the exact truth and so dances around the edges of the volcano.

Carl will grow up to be over six feet tall, with Eurasian eyes and curly hair kept in military trim. By the time he is thirty, he will have developed habits that will fascinate and later irritate his future ex-wife. He will travel to Bayreuth for the Wagner festival and attend twenty performances of the *Ring*. Every morning he will rise at dawn to listen to the BBC from his house in San Antonio, or his apple orchards in South Africa near Capetown or later in Washington State. He will routinely listen to Mexican radio to keep up his Spanish and will take tango lessons, moving awkwardly around the floor in his Brooks Brothers shirts and penny loafers.

All of his girlfriends before and after his divorce will say a version of the same thing. Carl loved to be touched. He needed that closeness. That's all he cared about. That was under everything. He wanted to connect. Despite what you might think.

The stage is set, soon enough we will live on opposite sides of the country. By then, we will have developed dossiers of grievances against each other. So many, so much. *Why did you write that? How could you have said that? Do you hear yourself?*

We are a family of letter writers, of furious typists in the middle of the night. In San Antonio, in our quiet suburb of emerald lawns, there is the hum outside of evening cicadas, and on Fridays, the cheers of the high school football game can be heard faintly from Alamo Stadium. Inside, we have our own peculiar music. Four manual typewriters, at a time before computers and electric Smith Coronas, bolted to typing tables, banging out from four different rooms, then wheeled back into the closet with their plastic covers pulled down tight. Sometimes we get glimpses of each other from behind the barricades.

We took our training with us on the road.

From Carl, in the first weeks of his college days, typed out from his dorm room at the University of Pennsylvania:

September 14
Dear Marie,
Only people from Brooklyn use the word Jeez. I am sure Mother coerced you into writing that mass of nonsense. Your letter does not have a single worthwhile sentence in it. I will not buy you

any notebooks. I repeat: No notebooks. But I will send you some
decals that are not to be placed in my room, around my room,
or on the window of my car.

He signed it with an elaborate flourish, in an inch-high triumphant scroll.

Gotcha! From the firstborn son.

I, even then at the age of fifteen, a collector of future useful information, noted carefully in the bottom left corner: "A letter from Carl Brenner, 1965."

My handwriting looped backward, scrunched together, a classic second-born, waiting for a shot.

AUTUMN 1967

I am seventeen and in my first weeks in college at the University of Pennsylvania. "Sgt. Pepper's Lonely Hearts Club Band" is on the airwaves, pot grows in the sinks at ZBT, and the girls of Hill Hall are not allowed visits from men except on Sunday afternoons, with the door left open and "if sitting on a bed, one foot on the floor." I have a Texas accent; two charm bracelets, one silver and another gold. On the silver one is a canoe from a camp in the Texas hill country. The trunk, which will follow me into my apartments in New York, Boston, London, and Los Angeles, has my name stamped in gold: Marie Harriet Brenner. It has as well a typed list of all the clothes it contains. "14 Pappagallo flats. 9 Villager skirts . . ." "If you are old enough to go to college, you can pack and go on your own," my mother says. "And you must inventory everything you own."

That autumn, and for years after, letters from my father arrive in flurries of envelopes with red, white, and blue air mail stripes. In the upper left corner is his company name, Solo Serve, printed on a trademark diagonal. The Store, as it is called in the family, is a local institution, a pioneer discount chain that sells a hodge-podge of trendy dresses, shoes, fancy cosmetics, and upholstery fabrics, all of them stamped with the Solo Serve tickets that say LOOK FOR DEFECTS. He takes the motto seriously and bangs out one hundred words a minute without a mistake.

"It just occurred to me that neither you nor Carl can spell. In your letter appeared ABSENSE and PREPERATION. . . . In his HURRICAINE and some other choice items. Am glad that you both write, however, and hope that I am not inhibiting you. . . . Who could?"

In October of 1967, he will turn fifty-six and has expanded our family's business. He now plans a year-long campaign against "the goddamn corrupt real estate people at our temple" who are trying to buy up a historic neighborhood to profiteer on a world's fair soon coming to San Antonio. Opinionated and cranky, he is a district attorney without portfolio, a room clearer in the gilded world of country club San Antonio. He has noted the facts of his life in a tersely written four-page memo that he keeps in a file marked "MCB Personal" but never shares. Included are the following: Born, Aguascalientes, Mexico, October 7, 1911. Matriculated the University of Pennsylvania, 1928, completed requirements, 1931, graduated second in his class at nineteen. In his twenties, fought and won "the biggest anti-trust price-fixing case in recent Texas history against the liquor monopoly winning $500,000 in 1940" and "was the youngest staff member in Hq. in Washington, Chief of Finance for the Air Transport Command, assisting C. R. Smith, President of American Airlines, to activate a world-wide transportation corps."

He had typed carefully: "Won numerous citations and commendations and was awarded the Legion of Merit [highest award in his field]."

Every age has its own language.

"You will do well in life if you learn to make a man feel important," my mother said, as she kissed me good-bye at the San Antonio Airport. "Always let them think they are the smartest!" And this: "You won't have an orgasm until you find the man you want to marry. Remember that."

In my first weeks at Penn, an elaborate box arrived from Frost Brothers, the Saks Fifth Avenue of San Antonio, with a dozen white panty girdles. "Wear these at all times and you will not send an invitation," my mother wrote on the card.

Like a czarina, Mother had instructions to cover all situations in life. "When you get to New York for Thanksgiving, order the oysters Rockefeller. Delicious! And very low in calories. Please call my sister. Do not charge any more phone calls!"

And this: "In New York, always take the elevator down, never up. You need to climb stairs, but if you meet a man on the way up, you will likely never see him again. On the way down, he will take one look at you and say, 'Let's go for coffee.'"

As I leave for college, my mother, at forty-four, quotes *Feminine Forever*, feels suddenly free, writes careful postcards to a flirty med school student she met by accident, cleans her closets, signs up for courses in psychology. She wears tweed Jackie knockoffs bought at Solo Serve and worries about Carl, at Penn, being drafted for Vietnam. "What is everyone writing and saying about the military?" she asks.

That spring vacation, I am home when she awakens me, tears streaming down her face. "My God, they've killed Martin Luther King. What do we do now?" Within weeks, she was organizing San Antonio Mothers for Peace and making plans to barge into the hotel room of Defense Secretary Robert McNamara when he came to San Antonio to give a speech. "If I look chic, maybe he'll let us in," she said.

The year 1967 was the twilight of a world of invisible webs.

My father wrote to me in the first weeks of college: "I am opposed to all fraternities and sororities as I think they make you move into too narrow a circle. . . . Someday as you travel more, you can study Asia or India or other thinking that will truly be new for you."

He was creating for me a view of myself, but I did not get it then.

He shuns all parties in San Antonio and types for hours after dinner. Dear Senator, Dear Congressman, Dear Mayor. He sends me the carbons and the photocopies, neatly clipped with a typed memo. *I showed the bastard!*

9

Years of letters, neatly filed.

I find them in a trunk in the basement stashed behind tennis rackets, ski parkas, and bikes.

"You kept all of these?" my husband asks, finding me in a sea of pastel valentines from the Johnson years, surrounded by files and scraps. "You have to be out of your mind to have kept this stuff." He is a futurist and can listen for hours to Hong Kong traders with Mandarin accents on conference calls on speaker in our kitchen. When I walk in, he will scribble a hasty note: "Here is the future! The world has changed!" I keep that note in a file marked "Ernie."

A paper trail will always set the record straight.

Setting the record straight is hardwired into the Brenner DNA.

10

I am a reporter. That means I am a magpie of facts, an issuer of sound bites, a repeater of opinions, an arbiter of everyone else's self-importance, ego blurts, and grandiosity, a sponge recycling reports from the front. I know whom to call in Afghanistan to get a fixer and who can take you into the troubled mosques in the *banlieues* of Paris. Reports from the front are our specialty, as is being able to recite with certitude what sounds like the new thinking on any and every subject from George Bush's pathology to the hidden landscapes of the brain. We journalists are often operating with assumptions based on misinterpretations, or soon to be irrelevant. We write, as is repeatedly said, first drafts of history.

From time to time I have worked in archives, sifting through the letters and papers of presidents and figures of history, looking for that tiny detail that can be held up, reinterpreted in search of a little-known fact or an illuminating story line. It's an odd and risky occupation, vicarious and thrilling, a way, many feel, to put the grid of someone else's life on your own complexities.

A hot September day. I've been at the wedding of a close

childhood friend's daughter in the hill country. The conversation is about the excesses being spent on the velvet gowns for next spring's fiesta queens. "Y'all look so great. Have you heard that Courtney has been chosen to be the Duchess of the Imperial Swan? Her dress is going to weigh 120 pounds."

"How thrilling," I hear myself say, suddenly sounding as Texas as my former high school friends. The sound of Jet Skis on Lake LBJ is the background hum of all those Texans with their roadie cups of margaritas, weaving up and down the lakefront beach.

On this weekend, there is a drumbeat of conversation about the coming calamities of Enron and Ken Lay. The word is beginning to circulate among these Texans that Enron is overextended, a house of cards, but little has appeared in the press.

"We hear that everyone in Houston is trying to sell their stock," one friend says. The South Texas crowd has sensed that Lay is an Elmer Gantry—the louche aspect of Houston and its displays of oil money. This does not sit well with the haute bohemian style of old San Antonio.

The next day I drive up to Austin in a hurry to get to the Harry Ransom Center, a vast research facility with the papers of Samuel Beckett, Don DeLillo, George Gershwin, William Faulkner—and my father's sister Anita, a plump girl with her nose pressed against the glass of socialist high society.

I've waited a long time to read the papers of my aunt. Until now, my cousin Susannah has had her mother's letters in a garage in Mexico City, changing the subject when I have called her asking to come down and see them. She's written her own book. *We Brenners wear good armor,* Anita wrote in her diary in 1927.

Anita fascinated me. She lived in a house in Mexico City with a Diego Rivera portrait of her son, Peter, holding a limp rope, as if playing tug-of-war with an invisible opponent. Susannah,

Peter's sister, refused to pose for Rivera, whom she called "the detestable fat man." Susannah and Peter were cousins I hardly knew. In Anita's garage were files of letters from Edward Weston, Trotsky, and Frida Kahlo, and the notes for hundreds of her articles. I understood only the barest outline of her life story and of course the scrim of her accomplishments.

This is what I knew: She was bold and fearless and ran away to Mexico from San Antonio when she was eighteen. That took balls if you were a Jewish girl in San Antonio in 1923. All around her, the young literati were breathing art and reading theosophy: Gurdjieff and Kahlil Gibran.

Her father insisted that Anita be monitored by the Mexico City president of the B'nai B'rith.

It became impossible for me to get the image of that girl in Mexico out of my head. *Not this again,* Casey tells me on the telephone when I tell her I am in the archive. *What is it with you and this search for the past? Mom, get a life.*

Small-boned, with dark, curly hair framing her almond eyes, Anita had an exotic prettiness that was undercut by a mean curved nose. She was intellectually dazzling—at nineteen she was already writing for *The Nation*—and in Mexico City to have her ticket punched as a free spirit. There she was a presence without being a reality; a girl with big plans, drawn to the power-players of art.

It was a time in Mexico of political and artistic ferment. Diego Rivera would soon set up scaffolding and paint revolutionary murals in the National Palace. Edward Weston, the aloof and self-absorbed Californian known in America for his photographic portraits, was ensconced in the capital with his lover, the sultry photographer Tina Modotti. I later wrote about all of this in an attempt to begin to understand how Anita did it.

For Anita and her friends, Mexico City was Paris with a Spanish accent—houses covered with bougainvillea; *pulquerias* filled with young lefties; huge political murals and garish tchotchkes. Arriving from San Antonio, Anita quickly became a central member of a group that included the painters José Clemente Orozco, Diego Rivera, David Siqueiros, and later Frida Kahlo. Soon Anita was employing Weston and Modotti, was celebrated by the Spanish philosopher Miguel de Unamuno, and became a confidante of Rivera and Kahlo. Working day and night on a catalog of Mexican art, she turned it into a sassy manuscript and used dozens of Weston photos to illustrate her larger theme—the Mayan and Aztec cultures that lurked behind all the art in Catholic Mexico. Her timing was impeccable. Café society in New York was getting a strong case of Mexico fever at the very moment Anita shipped a cache of photographs of works by Orozco, Rivera, and Jean Charlot to publish in her 350-page book on Mexican art, called *Idols Behind Altars*. It was to be her first and best accomplishment. She was twenty-four years old, but these young years in Mexico would become the mainspring that created her.

People in Mexico City remember a scandal of the 1950s. It was a time in her life when she was editing a magazine for tourists. The writer Budd Schulberg lived across from her office. Her days as a literary star had dimmed, but she had turned into a grand hostess, the center of a circle, the person to see when you got to Mexico. Schulberg would watch her pace from his terrace and stare off with no uncertain melancholy. Her marriage had come off the rails and she was a woman approaching fifty, getting ready to erupt at her brother, my father, over the terms of a will.

She was large in her absence, talked about frequently by the family who still spoke to each other. A local pundit named them "the battling Brenners" and my source for most Anita information had always been Dorothy, a younger sister.

Across town from Anita, Dorothy has a ballet barre in her

penthouse on Insurgentes. Her dachshunds run around while she practices *La Bayadère*. Sometimes her lover, Charles, warms up with "O dolci mani" from *Tosca* and all of that happy sound will bounce its way through lunch. Dance, Dorothy tells Carl and me. Always dance. Carl zones out, annoys the dogs, gets scolded by the maids, drops tortillas off the balcony, hurls fastballs in the Mexico traffic.

Dance.

It keeps you young.

You cannot be sad and dance.

Dorothy repeats the commands she hears from her teachers, who call her Señora Dorotea. Chassé! Chassé! She is forty-seven when she starts this and is working on the steps for *La Bayadère*. Rehearsing, she often wears a purple leotard and smokes a cigarette. The silver plumes bounce off the mirrors.

"Why do you even care about any of this?" my cousin Jaime asked me in 1972. "It is all such ancient history."

I had no answers to this. At twenty-two, I certainly could not have said, This is about Carl. I was in Mexico for weeks then, filling notebooks with a version of a backstory, using the Potemkin village of my father's brother and sisters as a way of trying to understand my own mysteries. I was in his tiny office at the *Mexico City News*, the English paper, trying to convince Jaime, then the paper's editor, that he should give me a summer job. I bombarded him with questions about the family. His father and my grandfather were brothers.

"Everyone knows your aunt Anita plotted the assassination of Trotsky with Diego Rivera," he said, still hungover from drinking too many copitas the night before. "Your grandfather stole his money from my father. Write that in your notebook!" he said, trying not to laugh. Then he added, "Why waste any more time with this? Move to New York and have a ball! That's what Anita did!"

On the way to Austin, my father's voice came back to me. When I would rebel, he would say, "Another Anita! Here we go again!" He did not mean this as a compliment.

On this perfect day in a Texas autumn, I firmly believe I am at last going to understand what happened in the childhoods of my father and his older sister that would start a family war. The term "coherent story" keeps popping into my mind. Family therapists call this the genogram, the laying on of family theory. My narrow focus is on Anita, thought by some to be the Gertrude Stein of Mexico. I saw her life as a series of images but had no idea what was behind the paint. Here it was, unspooling in my head, a collage of covers illustrated by Diego Rivera for her magazine *Mexico/This Month*, boxes of yellowing clips from *The New York Times*, headlines of articles in *The Nation*. It does not escape my notice that her writing doesn't make her as famous ultimately as her fleshy naked bottom, bared for the photographer Edward Weston on a rainy day in Mexico City in 1925. The image will be known in high circles as the Pear-Shaped Nude and will be auctioned off at Sotheby's with a $300,000 reserve price, make its way into the collection of the Museum of Modern Art, make Anita famous in her world, and, down in San Antonio, where my grandmother grinds gefilte fish, it will be the source of hand-wringing, eyeball rolling, and endless mystery.

The book, pushed together with tenacity and a droll writing style, propelled her into New York literary circles. By any standards, *Idols Behind Altars* was a triumph.

Think of it, I later tell Casey. *Your great-aunt.*

The smart set in New York was discovering serapes and Aztecs and twittering about the avant-garde muralists and painters pushing their frescoes out into the world. In May of 1929, five months before the stock market crash and the publication of *Idols*, Madison Square Garden was turned into the capital of ancient Mexico for a benefit called Aztec Gold. It was a huge ticket, with a cast of a thousand playing roles from Cortés to Montezuma—Florenz Ziegfeld was an Indian chief. Miguel Covarrubias—by then a star contributor to *Vanity Fair* and *The New Yorker*—and perhaps Anita, had a role in the drama.

Anita noted in her diary, "Richard Hughes flatters me by saying that our styles are alike. I now seem to be a successful young author and strangers often know me. . . . Which is gratifying."

And for her brothers and sisters, Anita became the powerful sibling who pushed the others off the stage. At this moment, in 1929, there were signs that trouble was brewing.

You are reading too much into this, Carl later tells me. *Diaries don't prove a case. Any lawyer will tell you that.*

A typed notebook in the archive has details of trips Anita made from Mexico City to San Antonio. She was, Susannah noted in her book, grinding away at three jobs to support herself. Later, she filed dispatches for *The Menorah Journal.* Solo Serve, perhaps the first discount store in Texas, had taken off, and the family now owned a summer cottage on the Gulf of Mexico, a few hours away. Anita returned from Mexico to see her family and discovered an empty house. Her brothers and sisters were "hardly aware of her existence," she wrote.

> There is so much money here, a little of it, without strings, would make me so happy, and it is not making anybody particularly happy as it is. Oh well. My comfort is that soon I will leave. It seems that I cannot find my place here at all. I always

come home in all good faith and wanting [to] like everybody and somehow the whole thing gets on my nerves horribly, I have to make an effort at sanity and control.

It had somehow never occurred to me that Anita, at twenty-two, could be so whiny, playing a big drama of rejection because her family was at their beach house basking in new money. I have files of pictures from this period—Isidor in his Panama hat in a fishing boat; Isidor posing at the Solo Serve roof garden theater, which featured, from Mexico, the Cavalcade of Stars. Isidor celebrating his leap-year birthday at the Majestic Theater, telling the *San Antonio Express-News* reporter, "Success is in every immigrant's hands."

What a windbag. In Mexico, Anita is trying to support herself turning out smart essays about the Jews of Mexico. That was in the archive too. "Not long ago I was dancing at the house of a friend with a young man who seemed quite Mexican in his speech, his manner, his appearance. Within a few moments, he had placed himself, Daniel Levy, with smiling courtesy 'at my service' . . ." In San Antonio, Milton and Dorothy wind their way through school, forced to listen to their showboating father bragging constantly about Anita. She wrote long letters home describing her conversations about Gurdjieff with her friends over morning coffees at Sanborns, then asked her mother to whip up copies of "robes de style" to wow her new friends Diego Rivera, Edward Weston, and Frida Kahlo. Within a decade, she would be in New York clocking in with a contract at *The New York Times Magazine* and her own column, "A Mind of One's Own," at *Mademoiselle*. She earned a Ph.D. from Columbia without ever having a B.A.; Isidor surely reminded her sisters and brothers.

For years I had boasted of being Anita's niece, but the truth is,

I hardly knew her at all. My father and his sister had stopped speaking when I was eight.

My aunt's books and magazines sat in a glass cupboard on a shelf in my mother's study. The copy of *Idols*, as it is called in the family, is signed to my father: "For my dear brother, comrade and friend Milton. Anita. September 1929."

"I don't want to talk about it," is what my father always said when I brought up the subject of Anita. "What do you mean, you don't want to talk about it? She's your sister!" My father would disappear into a rabbit hole.

I told myself I could attack this material with a reporter's detachment. Who didn't have arcs of dead space and unfinished business with his siblings?

I can say this because I have begun studying what experts now call sibling conflict—the vast emotional minefield of brothers and sisters. I have pored over the recent literature. And now I'm close to a journalist's dream, a laboratory of family struggle, documented in archive boxes. And my own family too. I want to investigate if sibling problems are passed down in families like blue eyes and brown hair. Did my father's rage at his sister impact my relationship with Carl? Or maybe our lineage of fractures was just a universal scenario? The norm? I have looked at books on patterns of birth order, sisters, older brothers, twins. Most are filled with case studies of an irritating type: "Julie and Mark were having relationship problems . . ." What I want to know about Julie and Mark is, what led them into the author's gaze? The lens into case studies of older brothers and younger sisters surely must include the backstory of everyone they have encountered and their own individual natures.

A research study on siblings breaks down the percentages: 52 percent of all brothers and sisters have a close relationship, 12 percent have no relationship, and 21 percent are something called "borderline." I am a borderline, defined by and against my brother, locked into some ancient and immutable feud. There is a moat around our conversations. Why? Why did we spend years locked in struggle with each other? I had to believe there was a chance that some of the answers could be found in the past, in letters and facts and research, in new interpretations of patterns held up to the light. I was operating with a strict sense of Freudian principles, that the past could yield insights and applicable truths, if only one understood the sexual rivalries, the aggression, the scant affection. I could spin out a sound bite that might make you think I knew what I was talking about, had read the experts on nurture and nature, birth order, peer influence, mirror neurons, attachment theory, DNA. I believed that the lengthy letters and carbons that would soon be placed in front of me would be a key in the lock, a map to guide me through the day-to-day of five siblings struggling to be individuals, barking and braying and yearning for so much from each other.

11

The elevator takes me to the fifth floor, where the librarian is working on filing crates of family papers that I have never seen before. "There are a lot of boxes here. Where do you want to start? Letters of the Brenner children, 1923 to 1940? Perhaps there?"

I've had to check my purse and everything I am carrying into a locker to be able to come into the reference room. I'm allowed a legal pad and sharpened pencils. I've written something at the top of the pad I've copied out of *The Wisdom of No Escape*: "Anything you can learn about working with your sense of discouragement or sense of bewilderment or your sense of feeling inferior or your sense of resentment." Later, when Casey sees this taped on her door, she says, "You are such a dork," and writes with a large blue pen over it: DORK.

The boxes are in front of me. I have some experience with this. I have written a biography of a publishing family using material from boxes like these, but now, suddenly, looking at my father's signature on letters he wrote in high school and college, I panic. Dear Henry, Dear Anita, Dear Dorothy, Dear Leah, Dear Mother, Dear Father. There are hundreds of them.

I pull out a letter from my grandfather Isidor to Anita, written soon after the publication of her book *Idols Behind Altars*, when she was twenty-four. It's a biographer's dream, crowded with implications about a father and daughter. Letters like this could run away with you, allowing a researcher to believe that every future vulnerability and faltering of confidence can be traced back to an angry outburst set down at a weak moment in a parent's life.

My grandfather starts off gently with a lengthy story about a sea captain and a first mate who defied an order, showed individual initiative trading fruit, and made a tidy profit.

Then:

> *This little story may illustrate our original understanding before you left for college. If you will remember, we have talked about it, and have also written you afterwards that I would see you through with the necessary expense providing that you would do nothing else but attend to your college work until you got your degree.*
>
> *Now then, as it turned out, you have taken on a load more than you can carry, as it is not normal for anyone to attend a college, write a book, and still have a steady position as you have at the Nation. It is true that it has brought you a lot of fame, and the same as the captain and the first mate, you probably have made more profit. But you have not complied with our agreement, and as you well know, we have to comply with the law of compensation, therefore you are paying with sacrifice, worry, nervousness, and very likely breakdown of your health if you do not become normal and attend to college only. . . . My advice would be that you should concentrate your entire time to your college work until you get your degree.*

In other words, he was pulling the carpet and taking her off the payroll.

Consider the letter further: This is what you say and do to a daughter who has broken into a private club, moved her life forward with such brio?

I close my eyes in the archive. Surely somewhere in these ancient letters I will find some flash of eternal wisdom, some new universal truth that can see me through Act III. There are numerous gaps in what I understand. My father's older brother, Henry, who once struggled as a reporter, was often laid low by melancholy, and wrote volumes on the history of the Inquisition and the Jews of Mexico. None of it was ever published. And then there was Dorothy, the bon vivant, opera buff, and sexy redhead who dragged us to the Bellas Artes to see the glass curtain made by Tiffany, each time we went to Mexico. "The largest in the world," she said. She wrote in great gushes of luscious prose—it was clear to me anyway that she was the Stendhal of the family, but she could never get out of her sister's shadow.

From the convent, she wrote:

You know as well as I, Anita, how hard it would be for us to live together. We are much too alike in temperament to ever be happy with such an arrangement. Of course, it could be managed and we could pretty much go our own ways, but to be quite frank, Anita, I am afraid of living with you. Yours is too dominant a personality and mine is too unresolved right now, and I am afraid that, unconsciously, I will become an imitator, an echo of you.

I am now tormented by my aunts' and uncle's urgencies, written in a flush of adolescent rage and yearning, all that young braininess and angst, coursing through Dorothy's college-age prose:

Life continues as bad as ever. The family is quite unbearable. Mama is quite unchangeable, and keeps on in her chosen method of being a mother by being just a Feeder. Meaning, of course, that the kids are super-barbarians, and that she keeps on being mindful only of not scratching the furniture, and scolding incessantly for no reason at all. Very pleasant. Henry is also the same. Absolutely settled into being disagreeable no matter what happens. Of course, I am also the same. Granted that I am thoughtless, and selfish, but still it is damn hard. I try to get along with them but I just can't.

They all seem to be so relieved when I go out to school, including Mama, that I cry for sheer bitterness. Silly!

Soon after, Dorothy ran away to Uruguay, then wound her way back to Mexico. Anita later interviewed Trotsky on the outskirts of Paris.

And then there was Leah, the youngest daughter, nicknamed Baby, who was put to work in the thirties tending to Diego Rivera as his secretary and go-between. Attacked in an assassination attempt on his life, she escaped from Mexico, had a fling, and got pregnant; the baby was given up in a private adoption the year Carl was born. Years later, I was startled by the man who tracked me down at my desk at *The New Yorker*. "I am the baby your aunt Leah gave up," he said.

I am expecting no new secrets and so I am not prepared for what I find. In a box marked "1960s," a small leather journal.

"I am at the end," it reads. "There is no reason to go on." Anita's handwriting is a fading diagonal. She is about to pinwheel into chaos, the bright promise of all those fading clippings in *The New York Times* morphing into something else, a mood that threatens to overwhelm her. Why is this journal in an archive?

And here are earlier letters from my father, chafing and pissy in Philadelphia, trying to struggle through the Depression, tutoring Dekes at the Wharton School:

Dear Anita,

. . . The work here is very hard, even in my case, as you know I have had a half year of work in the University of Texas. But I am not sorry I decided to come here, as the meeting of a different class of people and methods here is an education in itself. With the combination of these two factors, I suppose that I should be fairly well sophisticated at the end of four years of college work here. . . .

Write me soon and tell me something to tell you in the next letter.

He's seventeen and signing his letters to his own sister "Milton Brenner." He's driving her crazy wanting invitations to her parties. Their relationship is such that angling for attention from the Famous One, he's so nervous and sucking up around her that there it is, "Milton Brenner."

Suddenly, I am sobbing uncontrollably at the Harry Ransom Center, overwhelmed by how predictable everything that happened for the next fifty years surely was, how it was all right here, written, filed, kept in frayed manila folders: children born, love affairs and divorces, more children born, a world war—all of them now dead, but the snowflakes drifting through the galaxy of the family, as if a spigot had been turned on at a certain moment and can never stop.

The archivist looks up and says, "Are you all right?"

My voice is shaking as I try to make a joke. "I guess this kind of thing happens all the time, when the family members come to see their papers."

"No, honey," she says, her voice soft. "Actually this is a first."

I am still sobbing when I come out of the library. I call Ernie. "This is horrible," I say. "I will never go back there."

"Come home," he says. "New York is beautiful. There's a great weather forecast. We could drive out to the beach to take a walk."

"I can't," I say. "Carl is flying in from the harvest to Newark.

We're going straight to Columbia Presbyterian to check on a clinical trial. There could not be a worse day."

The next morning I awaken to see Jack Welch being interviewed on the *Today* show. He owned NBC and he's out pushing himself and promoting a book he's written about himself called, I write down, *Jack: Straight from the Gut*. Matt Lauer's in the saddle, putting him through a Q and A.

I am spending the morning in bed, waiting to get to the airport, still shaken by my discoveries in the archive. I have a thick stack of copies of Brenner letters next to me, pulled together in a frenzy. I'll read them on the plane, I think.

I look up to see the World Trade Center on the screen. The news of a small plane that has hit a tower. I call Carl immediately. It's before six a.m. in Wenatchee, but of course he'll already be up.

Matt Lauer looks startled, listening hard into his earpiece.

"Carl Brenner."

"You may have a problem getting into Newark," I say. "Some little plane has buzzed the World Trade Center."

"Don't worry about it. I'm out with the pickers now." He sounds irritated I've made the call. "I've gotta go."

A few minutes after eight a.m. I call him back. "Another plane has hit the towers. They think it might be a terrorist attack."

"Look," he says, "I will be at Newark. You may change your plan—that's what you do. Not me. I'll get there. Don't you worry about it." His voice shakes with rage.

"You have to get to a TV. A radio. America is being attacked," I say, and hang up.

Within minutes, the telephone rings. "I have reconfirmed my appointment," he says, satisfaction in his voice.

"I don't think you understand," I said. "America is under attack." I can hardly speak.

"Why do you always exaggerate everything?" he screams.

1 2

· ·

This is my version of the subsequent events.

NEW YORK CITY
OCTOBER 7, 2001

A Sunday, balmy, with more than a hint of autumn in the air.

I am running away from New York, running to my brother, unaware that a crevice is about to open up in my life. My papers and e-ticket and cell phone and BlackBerry are all over the seat in a taxi on the way to the airport, and I am fighting a wave of dizziness, convinced that I will miss the plane. "You know there could be two hours getting through security," the driver says. "La-Guardia is a madhouse." The woman in the taxi making frenzied calls on her cell could be a lawyer consulting with a client, a reporter on a story, or anyone who feels as if she is out of time.

"Where are you going?" the driver asks.

"To Washington. The state. Where they grow the apples," I say, annoyed that a stranger talks to me. What I do not say is that I am on the way to visit my brother.

The conversation stops cold. I radiate tension, that leave-me-alone quality of the frenzied New York woman in black, as if no one else has a situation that is more crucial than mine.

October is not a month when under normal conditions any city person likes to leave New York and certainly not for the apple country, tucked away in the Cascade Mountains. The city comes alive after a hot, sleepy summer, but not this year. I carry a large canvas bag of research. There is nothing unusual about this. I often travel with files on someone I am set to interview. I have folders marked "Apples" and "Orchard Systems" and "Family." I have as well my reporter's tools—tape recorders, legal pads, and a box of fine-point pens. In the folders there are pamphlets on orchards and how to prune and plant them, the history of fruit growing in Washington State. I have already learned that the first apple trees in Wenatchee were planted in 1872. There is a darling book I have checked out of the library called *All About Apples* that has cute drawings of red and gold apples in pen and ink.

Something is wrong here. Even I know that.

I am treating my brother as if he is a source, someone I have been assigned to interview. I am acutely aware that this is not normal, trying to master the material, to learn facts and appropriate apple country sound bites on my way to visit my older brother, but I am panicky, convinced that I must appear smart.

Carl has owned orchards in the apple country since Ronald Reagan was president. On these two hundred acres are 100,000 trees that produce Galas and Braeburns and Goldens and tart perfect red Jonagolds. There are Bartlett pears and Taylor's Golds and Anjous and a cornucopia of reds—Red Chiefs, Red Stripes, and an odd variety called the It, grown by a neighbor friend, that is about the best red you can eat.

The question that I have been unable to answer is how is someone who is so weird and difficult able to grow such delicious fruit?

Carl does not like surprises. He makes plans months in advance and then gets furious if anyone—me, for example—changes them. He did not attend either of my weddings because I changed the dates for reasons that I can no longer remember. I already made other plans, he said. He was going to hear the *Ring*. *You would miss my wedding for Wagner?* I said.

I decide I will not tell my brother I am coming. One morning I get up and say to Ernie, "I am flying to Washington State and will not be back for weeks. I hope you do not have a problem with this." I spend the day running around New York City buying what I consider to be orchard-appropriate clothes—fleeces and jeans and oversized denim shirts, the kinds of cotton turtlenecks I wore in college. I cross Central Park to shop at Patagonia on West Eightieth Street and try, in my paranoid post-9/11 state, not to freak out at every fire truck or ambulance or police siren I hear. I have already bought duct tape and painter's masks for the house and a miniature battery-operated TV at Best Buy for $200. That morning I spend some hours online trying to find an inflatable boat because a friend is convinced that the only way we can escape New York when the next attack comes will be the East River. "Forget Abercrombie and Fitch! Forget all of the places downtown! I have been everywhere and no one has them."

It seems that every phone conversation begins with, "Are you okay?" I am not okay and neither is anyone else I know. I drive to Providence to see Casey, a sophomore at Brown. In the middle of the quad is a board where students can write about their feelings. And of course there are hundreds of pictures of the dead, two of whom we know. One young woman, just out of Princeton, had started her job that month. Casey and her best friend, Rachel, shake with nerves, then deny anything is wrong. I immediately burst into tears.

"Please don't do this," Casey says. "You are not dying. We are safe. *Safe*."

For days I am at the press center set up at the Westside pier. By the third week, the losers and self-promoters from all over find their way here and are setting up with their guitars, strumming songs about redemption, hoping to catch a mention in a magazine. There are fights every day among the reporters to see who can get on a launch to be taken down to the acrid shell where squads of firemen are pulling charred remains out of the rubble. People I know are bragging that they have "been up all night" serving meals to firemen. Henry Kissinger shows up in the ruins and calls a press conference. He wears a red tie and a somber pin-striped suit.

"It changes you for life," Rudy Giuliani says, in his New York Yankees cap.

"Rudy is here every fifteen minutes," a reporter from *New York* magazine whispers.

"God bless you," the mayor says to the firemen, and then Kissinger and Rudy go off to look at a building with burnt-out windows that, they tell the small group around them, had been built in 1888. When I get off the launch, the face of George Bush is looming over the podium in the press room. "The Taliban has beheaded 100,000 people. We will stop them," the president says, his eyes squinched to dots.

Suddenly it feels like the clock is running out. I had a belief that Carl, who was never glad to see me, would somehow be glad to see me and that I could get beyond this canyon of rage that defined us for reasons that were wholly mysterious to both of us. I put away the fleeces and the jeans and wear what I always wear—a black turtleneck, black slacks, and flats. "Black cashmere at the orchard?" Ernie says as I leave for the airport. "Carl will not like that."

13

Here, on the day I fly from New York, is an image I cannot shake: My brother Carl stands in his boxers and looks out a grimy window at darkness. At this moment, he is in search of a miracle and wakes at dawn, age fifty-four, in a motel room in the middle of the apple country, alone and filled with dread. He is not thinking about New York. On this first pass, I see him as I, younger sister, perceive him to be. It does not occur to me that Carl might in fact prefer to be alone in a motel room, elated to have every annoyance, e-mail, beeping telephone, plumber, electrician, cut down to a single thrilling retreat for only $45 a night.

Who would ever understand?

He keeps it secret, everything he feels. It is here that he zones out, goes to silence, dreams. He is overcome with the wonder of possibilities, of expanding through the Columbia Valley and perhaps even taking on hundreds of acres once owned by Dole. And of mastering an entire new breed.

He's made a choice.

It's written on a file in the middle of his desk.

The Honeycrisp.

They love the light.

How can he, the Howard Roark of fruit, explain to anyone about the light?

The dogs bark in the orchards. That is the only sound you hear.

And this: a banging screen door in Cashmere. Sadot, his farm manager. *Hola*, Señor Carl.

And then the harvest.

Not a moment to spare. Up at four a.m. and in the fields with the pickers as dawn breaks. The sound of their ladders in the trees, the plop of the fruit in the bags. Sometimes they sing: *Es la historia de un amor.*

He struggles to remember the words.

To bring it back.

Everything.

Room 278 of the Hawthorn Inn. The room overlooks a parking lot, a railroad track, and a sign company with a pink and purple neon sign that blinks on and off: GRAYBEAL SIGNS. He can hear trucks rolling down Wenatchee Avenue, the sound of the four a.m. train headed for Seattle. By sunrise, the ten-wheelers will be up and down Highway 97 through the necklace of farm towns that lie along the Columbia River.

Five a.m. The pink light has yet to come over the Cascades. Already at the Big Y in the town of Peshastin, the growers are ordering a farmer's special, a sausage and cheese and ham omelette the size of a snowshoe. It is a ritual, these early breakfasts at the Big Y, from the days when the apple kings ruled the Cascades and the Washington Red was the very symbol of America and the richness of its land.

At the top of Carl's to-do list is the phone call he waits to make. Stuck to the top of the list is a large yellow Post-it on which is written again the single word: Honeycrisp.

Much later, when I try to re-create what was on my brother's mind that day, October 7, 2001, I will draw on my usual reporter techniques. I will type "Honeycrisp Apple new variety" into Google and 123 entries will pop up. I will make notes on the facts of the variety. I will try to put together a plausible account.

Among the facts I culled are the basics: The Honeycrisp is a new variety of apple developed by a breeder at the University of Minnesota. His name is David Bedford. That name had appeared on one of my brother's lists in the Orchard box. Researching Carl's apple life seemed a reasonable method to enter his strange world, to see him as he might have been.

No one in the family knew what to make of Carl and his apple life. It was 1982. Carl was then a trial lawyer, complaining about the tedium of litigation. He announced it one night at dinner, "I've bought some orchards," he said. "In Africa. I'm going to learn the fruit business." You could hear that little silence on the telephone whenever the subject of his orchards came up. That's the way our family worked, as if nothing was amiss. He was soon to be married and was keeping what he was doing in a separate trust, already thinking about what he would do if he eventually divorced. "You cannot be too careful," he said. I had introduced him to his future wife, a stylish young magazine editor I had interviewed for a column. "You should meet my brother," I gushed in a restaurant on Lexington Avenue. She had a great laugh and said, "I'd love to." It was a moment that became thirteen years in my brother's life. He later used the word "mistake" and would change the subject when her name came up. The rupture was painful, and whatever happened between them was never discussed. My younger-sister urge-to-please phantasms carried me away. Was I just trying to make conversation? I was thirty-two and reading books about creativity, underlining Julia Cameron's *The*

Artist's Way. I was trying to start my mornings speed-writing in a journal, as Cameron suggests. My future sister-in-law was as well a rapid diarist who had grown up in Louisiana and once studied with Walker Percy. She did not mention much about her family except the fact that she had lost her mother when she was young.

"Apples?" my mother said to Carl. "This sounds like a joke. What is this about? Back to the shtetl? My son, the Jewish Johnny Appleseed?" Punctuated by her flirty laugh. It was her way to paste you under the niceness. He sent pictures of his first days in Wenatchee, kneeling by the plantings of the whips, the tender shoots of trees. *Lovely,* she said. Always that. *Lovely.* She treaded lightly, deferential and disguised, years of complexities tabled, filed in the catalog of *Let's move on*. Carl's marriage was in that file as well.

On October 7, 2001, Carl has written on a white legal pad, the following question: *Why are these apples so great?*

That will be his lead-off question for Bedford. He tells me that later, after the call has been made. I note it carefully in a journal. Like everything with Carl, the tone is off and open for misinterpretation. Had I been there, I would have said that such a question—*Why are these apples so great?*—needed lightness, even whimsy, a little topspin on the ball. I would have said that asked the wrong way, the question could offend, could imply that the asker thought the opposite. I would have said, How can you ask a question like this?

He has written out the questions carefully on the legal pad: Stony or sandy soil? Climate? Nitrogen? River effect? Would the Honeycrisp be easier to grow in Chelan with its balmy sunshine by the lake? The term used for the variety was "grower unfriendly." It was hell to cultivate. The Honeycrisp was an unpredictable variety for the Cascades. How to get the sandy soil of the high desert to accept it? There was the matter of the thin skin of the fruit, the shortness of the stems, the tiny shears the pickers needed to get them off the trees. The Honeycrisp was likely to get the acne of fruit known as bitter pit.

David Bedford has an unusual occupation. He is an apple specialist, a fruit imagineer who plays around with varieties. Apple trees can be magical inventions; each one can be a melting pot of a breeder's design. You can crossbreed and pollinate, chance into freak mutations and then be unable to duplicate them. You can graft together entirely different apple trees as if you were adopting another family system to take root in your own. All of the grafts and the budding and the pollination, but you could wind up with mutations, fruit that was completely different from what it was predicted to be. There are experimental stations in Japan and Australia, labs where apples can be developed that taste like chocolate or licorice or are the size of olives. Apple varieties can take thirty years to develop.

Bedford had started working on the Honeycrisp when he was just out of grad school and Carter was president. At this moment, there are people at Cornell University who are competing ferociously with apple breeders in Washington State, and having their clocks cleaned by the guys in New Zealand and Japan, although Bedford would disagree. I will later learn all this as well. Bedford had a long history of breeding and crossbreeding and frequently took calls from reporters and orchardists who wanted to understand his methods. Over the course of his career he had gone nowhere with his SnowSweet and Zestar! One day he got the idea to play around with some trees marked "Discard" from his experimental grove. The next year he was floored by the apple's texture and taste. And now, thirty years later: the Honeycrisp.

The desk at the motel is covered with Carl things, meticulously stacked and labeled with yellow Post-its in order of importance. The legal pads with their lengthy to-do lists are written carefully in a lawyer's hand in blue ink—a Cross ballpoint pen presented to him when he earned a high score on the Texas bar exam in 1972. He has posted a sign on his wall: A FAILURE TO PLAN IS A PLAN TO FAIL. He writes the lists at night, in the morning, and all throughout the day, then puts a line through each item completed, phone call made, letter mailed. Also on his desk is a stack of printouts on which Carl has circled "explosive taste" and "sweet and tart" in a pamphlet sent by the breeder touting the wonders of this new miracle fruit. It is a firm-fleshed crunchie that explodes with sweetness, an American invention. Planting the new varieties from Japan annoys the patriot in Carl, and he wonders who the hell would ever go into a grocery store and demand a Tsugaru?

This morning the front page of *Wenatchee World* has a headline: "U.S. Troops on the Move." Carl notices it at dawn. And underneath: "Published in the Apple Capital of the World and the Buckle of the Power Belt of the Great Northwest." Carl is trying to ignore Paula Zahn and the endless footage of the collapsing towers, the images of New York in crisis, to get to the details of his day. He has taken a position on Zahn and will hold forth on her later at McGlinn's, announcing that it is his opinion that Zahn is "way out of her depth on this jihad thing." For that matter, no one understands the president and how he is doing a damn fine job under grueling conditions, that he is "a born leader" and is the right man for the right job at the right time.

He makes phone calls from the lobby of the motel, brings shopping bags of bottled water and almonds and chocolates to his room to avoid the minibar. The shoes are lined up in his closet, his shirts color-coded, even at the Hawthorn Inn. He has a wooden footlocker in the room and in it are the waders for the damp walks through his orchards, his laptop, his padded beige vests, and a shotgun.

He has already laid out his breakfast—fruit bread from the

Anjou Bakery on Highway 2. He stops in every day on his way to his orchard in Cashmere, hoping to make conversation with the owner, who grew up in Seattle and whom Carl believed went to cooking school in Tuscany, a few miles from the *David* and the Japanese tourists making their way to the Ferragamo outlets. Sofia, the owner's assistant, has displays of porcini mushroom tarts, flourless chocolate cakes, marionberry pies. She is, additionally, a daily reader of the *Times*, but even more important, she uses language he understands, such as "care with fruit." This is said reverentially to describe a person with a small-farm sensibility, often a dot-com dropout who has migrated east from Seattle. Whatever Carl thinks of her granola politics, anyone who loves fruit is okay with him. Outside the Anjou there is a stand with perfect purple fingerling potatoes and exquisite golden plums. Carl has developed a degree of friendship with the platoon of people he encounters every day; it passes for intimacy. He knows the name of the woman who wears the cotton gloves to pack his fruit at the Hi-Up company in the town of Peshastin. He is aware, although he discourages the conversation, that Bob, the plump and sweaty deskman at the Hawthorn, has fallen in love with the local massage therapist. He can feel that Bob wants to engage him on this topic as he makes his way out every morning at dawn, passing the checkerboard set up on the lobby table, the checkers large red and green sponges in the shape of apples. Carl is always in a hurry and barely hears the swimmers in the indoor pool, does not take in the chlorine smell piercing his nostrils.

He takes the fruit bread out of its Ziploc bag and saws a piece off with a serrated knife he brought from his house in Texas. Before he toasts the bread, he puts the loaf back in the bag. As a child, he kept a sign on his door instructing everyone to remove his or her shoes before entering his bedroom. Even then his shirts were organized by color, the shoes carefully polished every night.

He liked to think of himself as an eight-year-old, carefully work-ing on the leather, bringing it to a high gloss—the satisfaction this brought him, the sense of order and mastery. "It is all about the details," he tells his friends. "How did John McCain survive those camps?"

And on his desk this morning, the following, clipped from the *Seattle Times*: "Apple Growers Are Calling It Quits" and an editorial, "An Apple Crisis: Time to Be Creative." The editorial opined, "Give up the Red Delicious as the emblematic apple. Promote the better-tasting species. Put some romance in it. Sunkist did it. Ocean Spray did it." All those commands, as if he missed the theme.

And for what? The Jazz? The Pink Lady or the Cameo? He is a minor player in the war of the varieties. He worries over the question: Why has America turned away from its apple master-piece, the Washington State Red Delicious? When did it turn into this overproduced pulpy mess? He could understand the diehards who still search for Russets with their cloying sweetness, but never the Gala and Golden crowd. He later that day drives to his three orchards, west toward Cashmere, passing the sign for the Aplets & Cotlets candy factory, then doubles back toward Chelan. There, he has lunch by the lake with Grover Collins, a packer who reminds him of our father, and bombards him with ques-tions about what the apple country was like when Collins was a young man and the apples were shipped east in wooden boxes made by hand. Collins started that way, nailing boards together during the Depression. Now Reggie, his son, runs Chelan Fruit, one of the largest packinghouses in the region. His is an all-American story, and Carl broods on this as we travel on to the town of Pateros, a few mountains down the highway. NPR cuts in and out of the Cascades, and the light dapples over the purple foothills as he tries to hear how it is going in Afghanistan. "Those damn lefties," Carl tells Sofia. "How is it a liberal position that the

Microsoft crowd can send *their* kids to college but an apple farmer can't sell his land because of their goddamn zoning laws?"

The apple country is the real America, Carl often said. Everything was here, if only the Seattle crowd and the people in Washington, D.C., would see it.

14

You could not understand Carl unless you understood his farm manager, Marc Armstrong. That much I knew. On the morning of October 2, 2001, Marc is in the middle of an orchard in Pateros, which is real farm country, as opposed to farm country where there might be an occasional yoga studio. Pateros is a bend in the road with miles of apples and pears in the Methow Valley, terracing the cliffs of the river. You can stop at two churches or the Rest Awhile fruit stand, where the pies are out of the oven by eleven a.m. Carl has arranged to have his *Wall Street Journal* delivered to the Rest Awhile since the mail carriers will not drive from farm to farm. Pateros is where Marc Armstrong presides over Carl's Boscs and Bartletts and Galas, waking up in a small green house with a picture window that overlooks the entire apple valley. He attends Sunday services at a meetinghouse in Brewster—which twice a year receives the satellite feed from Salt Lake City—and strictly observes Family Monday.

Carpe diem, Carl told the young Mormon who had answered a classified ad he placed in *Wenatchee World.* He was looking for "a hard-working individual" to manage his orchards, as if anyone would advertise for someone lazy. The ad had the social skills of a blowtorch.

Armstrong, husky and fair, resembles the round-faced Tom Sawyer whose face appeared on the Pride O'Washington apple box. His father worked a farm in Quincy, not far down the valley. He had never been to an opera, seen New York, or thought twice about the *Wall Street Journal*. Moreover, he was not so sure about this job, made uneasy by Carl's ad and what he had already heard in town. People said that Carl had a way of speaking that made you think he disliked you, that you were guilty and mistaken before you even ventured an opinion.

On the day they met in 1993, they looked over the valley in Pateros where Carl's orchard was soon to have 100,000 trees. Carl made a case for himself. He used the word "transformation" and the term "largeness of vision." "We will build something important here," he told Marc.

And then again, *carpe diem*.

Marc had first learned the term when he heard Robin Williams say it in *Dead Poets Society*. He looked it up when he got home: Seize the day. Now they were picking Braeburns and Goldens in Chelan and, later that week, they would start on the Boscs and Galas. There, Carl would walk among his trees, looking out to the valley, the lines of his orchards, stark, white, precise. Pickers had come from Oaxaca and Guanajuato, working their way up through the orange groves of California in early summer to the cherries and blueberries of Oregon until it was September and apple season in Washington. The apples would plop into their canvas bags in a method that had not changed since Herbert Hoover was in the White House. Ladders in the trees, bins in the fields. And my brother checking each piece of fruit for imperfections, bruises and blemishes and wens.

From his window, he sees the smoke. Another orchard in

flames. The purple flume is just visible in the dawn. It is so faint it could be a shadow, a reflection, a mirage. From this distance it is impossible to tell where the smoke is coming from. He must get Marc on the cell phone and see if he has heard anything. Five-sixteen a.m. Too early to call David Bedford in Minnesota, but Marc, he knows, has long been up.

15

Somewhere over Chicago, I begin to read *Good Fruit*. It's an oversized glossy published for apple growers, the *Vogue* of fruit. The issue I have has a photo of an apple orchard with neat rows of spindly trees in a lush green field in front of jagged mountain peaks. As it happens, it is one of Carl's orchards. It is a beauty, no doubt about it. There is a long white trellis where the trees have been trained to form an archway for a more efficient method of picking fruit. The orchard borders a state park used by rock climbers who come up from Seattle in their SUVs to take in the "Big Window"—the panorama of the Cascade Loop. You can buy the postcards with this vista—the vast grandeur of the Columbia Valley, the Columbia River a ribbon beneath the trees. The orchard commands the valley, a lucky find for Carl, the sun and the water combining to give ideal growing conditions for pears. I have been to this orchard once, then turned around and fled after thirty-six hours, driving straight through the Blewett Pass through the Bavarian tourist town of Leavenworth, where the yodeler at the Enzian Inn awakens guests with a Swiss horn.

My spirit returned only when I saw the Starbucks at the Seattle airport by the gate for the flight to New York.

What occupies me on this flight is how I am going to spend the next weeks with my brother. How to make light conversation about the king bloom and nitrogen sprays? Seasonal varietals? The Honeycrisp? What would we talk about? What was a "titi-vated tree"? We are strangers whose occasional meeting ground is in South Texas, or, even less often, in New York City when Carl comes to visit, though those encounters are usually brief, punctuated by a certain Carlness, a tension, a list of appointments and operas and restaurants he has booked, with the atmosphere at any moment ready to turn. A part of that visit would be a concern about what to do in our favorite neighborhood restaurants if Carl pays the bill. "How many glasses of wine did you have?" he has asked more than one guest. When it came time to leave the tip, Ernie would turn pale, it was so cheap.

Somewhere over Minnesota, I suppose, I brace myself for the conversation: *The president is doing a damn fine job at a tough time.* I will force myself to ignore the National Rifle Association sticker on the truck.

I have developed a socially acceptable answer when someone asks me if I have any siblings.

"Oh, yes," I say.

"Are you close?" I might be asked.

"We speak once a week," I say. Then I change the subject.

I have whittled my relationship with Carl to elegant minimalism. We employ the mantra of the Brenner family: We are so busy. Very busy.

My voice would assume a forced warmth:

How are the orchards?

Oh, fine.

The tightness in his voice is not masked by his excess of politeness, a certain custodial older brother quality.

But on this flight, I am determined to get along with him, to have him glad that I came to see him, flying across the country in a state of panic.

The trip to Wenatchee takes half a day. There is the endless flight to Seattle and then a drive across the state, through forests of pine trees and the Pacific Northwest fog. If there is snow on the Blewett Pass, you will not get through the mountain and will have to stay in the godforsaken town of North Bend. Or you can take a small Horizon Air plane into the apple country capitals—Wenatchee and Yakima. That connection can take hours, allowing you to make notes on the Pacific Northwest wardrobe color choice—faded raspberry and muted moss—not to mention the T-shirts, shorts, and Birkenstocks. Was there some universal bleaching agent in the Pacific Northwest water that faded out all colors?

I have plenty to read on the plane. I am asked from time to time, Are you a teacher? A lawyer? This is not how I see myself, but I must radiate a certain competence. I hide behind questions. Interviewing is what I do. I know what a psychiatrist would say: I am using questions as my shield. Is that fair? I am also genuinely curious. The reporter is there, like blue eyes and auburn hair.

Why can't I just be easy with my brother, the way I am with my friends? That we are not close seems a badge of shame, a personal failure, a mark of my inabilities, bossy nature, and tendency to exaggerate. Carl thinks of me as the human flaw.

I am going to give you a quiz.

This is how Carl starts many of our conversations.

I wish I were kidding.

16

College days. Carl is a senior and I am a nervous freshman, trying to impress. I eat roast beef sandwiches at midnight with girls who went to boarding school. I inhale six-packs of beer and stuff myself with peanut M&M's and Cheez Whiz. I've discovered coffee yogurt. My mother sends me letters telling me of her diets, her writing down every calorie, and her need to keep it to one thousand. She thinks I will not get the point.

I have a turquoise suede miniskirt and sit in the dorm snack bar with girls from the East Coast. One of my sorority sisters takes the train to New York on Fridays and returns on Mondays with shoe boxes attached with a string. They are from a swanky store on Madison Avenue, Lady Continental. The girls I go to school with wear black turtlenecks and jeans. I still wear pink pantsuits and a fall.

"I'm going to Vietnam," Carl says. We have dinner on Sunday nights at a Chinese restaurant on Spruce Street. "I am going to kill the gooks. I am going to be a jet bomber pilot. Daddy is having a breakdown. You have to back me up on this. Tell them it's a good idea."

"That's ridiculous," I say, spooning my Dannon yogurt,

which I eat only in front of Carl so that he will report to our mother that I am trying to lose weight.

He's wearing a black eye patch over his left eye. "This is the way I am strengthening my bad eye," he says. "My eyes aren't good enough yet to pass the eye test." Then, "You look fat. You better not let Mama see you like this."

At Christmas when I get off the plane, my mother bursts into tears.

Race riots take over Philadelphia. It is a time of extreme anger in America. A student is murdered on campus. Frank Rizzo, then police commissioner of Philadelphia, sends buses filled with cops that circle Spruce and Walnut. Within the year, the campus will be shut down by protesters. I wear a fringed jacket that has peace buttons on the sleeve. Carl shouts, "You are a Communist!"

Since high school, he has had a secret political life. He was the only teenager in San Antonio who carried a membership card to the John Birch Society, an organization of right-wing crazies that harped on the evils of the Soviets. Does he really believe all of this? His room in San Antonio was filled with manuals of alleged Communists published by the John Birch Society. I played Joan Baez records loudly to annoy him. One day, I came home from school to find them smashed. "She's a subversive," he said. "I have it right here on my list." None of this behavior was remarked upon in our house. It was just taken in, accepted as some kind of weird normal, not a larger sign of anything else but a mark of his individual nature.

"He's a freak," I tell my friends.

Carl walks me back to my sorority house, next to where he lives at his fraternity. "Take a look at this," he says. We walk in and there sit a row of bleached deer antlers still pink with blood from his weekend of hunting in the country. "I'm donating them to the house," he says, puffed up again.

He fails his eye test and never gets to Vietnam, instead enlists in the marines. At boot camp, in Quantico, the officers are trained to run through smoke and fires.

I remember all of this on the airplane to Washington.

The folder marked "Apples" has the seasonal trends, world-wide apple conditions, and lists of exports from China to Mexico that are killing the Washington apple farmers. I make my own list of new varieties with all their alluring names: Ambrosia and Arlet, SunCrisp, Williams' Pride. Then there are the new entries from the Japanese: Yatoke and Yataka and the Sansa. Under the list of Braeburns are a platoon of family names: Eve, Hillwell, Joburn, and Lochbuie.

The Van Well Nursery, a Wenatchee landmark, features apples on "Bud 9"—another unknown apple term for my list. The names draw me in: Ruby Jon, Golden Delicious, Manchurian Crab, Mutsu, Snowdrift Crab, and the Liberty. Soon, the names cover an entire page: Valstar, Finata, Buckeye Gala, Oregon Spur. There are dozens of names in each category of fruit. What would my life be like if I knew how to grow a nectarine? I don't know a damn thing about apples or, for that matter, how to deadhead a geranium. I am an imbecile when it comes to the dreary day-to-day activities of rural life. Growing apples is a bewildering occupation: How do you choose among Jonathans and Red Fujis and Red Staymans? Or Winesaps, Gravensteins, Royal Empires, or my personal favorite, the Rubinettes? How can anyone read this stuff?

"We will assume that your performance goals for an orchard management system are relatively high early production and fruit of the highest quality for the intended market."

That is the unspeakably dull opener of "Selecting the Right Orchard System" that I now highlight in yellow, selecting key terms—"integrated components" and its subcategories: the vertical axis, the Tatura Trellis, Lincoln Canopy, and something called Güttingen V.

Soon I have three pages of questions ready for Carl: How do you train a tree? What does "sunlight management" mean? What the hell is Güttingen V? Plant one thousand trees an acre or five hundred trees an acre?

I close my eyes. My friends are trying to take off for Afghanistan, to smuggle themselves into the Himalayas, hide Portacams under their burkas to report on the Taliban.

And what am I doing here, exactly?

An apple term jumps off the page from my reading: chance seedling. I have no idea what this means, perhaps something like my brother and me, two different apples coming from the same tree. The "chance seedling" term is in an article that I have brought with me, a photocopy from the *Encyclopaedia Britannica*, 1974 edition. I found it in the hush of the upstairs readers' room at the New York Society Library on East Seventy-ninth Street. I have spent much time there lately, pulling out dusty volumes of encyclopedias. I could obtain the exact same information by punching "apple" and "Encyclopaedia Britannica" into Google, but then I would be home, worrying about how to get duct tape to seal my windows and doorways, staring at CNN. The library is a haven of old New York: marble steps, nineteenth-century prints of the New York waterfront. The elevator is in a rickety cage that has not changed since 1917. You could sit at a readers' table and pull out the drawers, be reassured by the yellowing cards of entries, writing what you wanted on a slip with a nubby pencil.

17

Eleven a.m.: I settle in at the café across from the Horizon Air gates and fan out the newspapers on a green Formica table that overlooks a runway. A parade of small white planes with brown roadrunners on their sides fly to the apple country, then take off through the Pacific Northwest and up to Alaska. It is border country, preferred by hikers and the Unabomber, a route once taken by Lewis and Clark, alien from city life. I try to pony up some enthusiasm for the American frontier spirit and quickly return to the *Times*. I will call him after I finish my second coffee, work my way through a few biscotti. An hour passes. I now have a stack of newspapers in front of me. I reach into my purse to see three checkbooks, all with notes scribbled on the back. A wire connected to my Walkman trails on the airport linoleum. "Hey, you have a wire dangling," a man next to me says when I get up. He had just come from Patagonia, where he stayed in a motel that cost $8 a night. Within minutes, I know that he is a nurse who works in a mental ward in Seattle and lives with a Reiki instructor who had studied whales to treat people going through "life trauma cycles." I write the phrase in my notebook.

Carl will think it is weird if I just show up. I buzz with nerves, convinced that he will be angry. At the airport there is a tiny lounge where one can get a back massage. I settle myself into a chair. I have with me a tattered paperback called *Sibling Revelry* bought used from Amazon in preparation for the trip.

On page 134, there is an assignment. *Consider the following questions: What topics are taboo? At what point does communication come to a halt between you?* For a moment, I remember a story a friend told me about his own sister. She once kidnapped their mother at gunpoint and demanded that she sign checks to her and her husband before they would release her. This is extreme behavior by any standard. In comparison, Carl and I have an impeccable relationship. What topics are taboo? How about: his divorce and our parents? Under the classification of parents there was our father, or, Carl used to call him, "my father," which he used in sentences like, "You will not be allowed to call my father's doctors," as he was dying. And then there was our mother or "your mother"—the term he used when he explained to me some hours after she died that he had not thought to call me until her body was out of the house although I was asleep around the corner because, "You should have been there when your mother died." There was additionally our childhood in San Antonio unless it is a shared experience delivered with a comic punch.

A gray-shaded box neatly crosshatched in high-contrast is called: An Emotional Grid of Possibilities. The box asks a question:

What response can you have with a sibling?

1. I can be totally real, myself.

2. Sometimes real.

3. I'd sooner walk the plank or chew metal than truly be myself with my sibling.

I reach for my cell phone.

"Carl Brenner," he says. He always answers like that, as if he has crucial business to attend to

"Surprise. I am in Seattle."

"You are in Seattle? What are you doing there?" I am startled and delighted: Carl sounds happy that I am here.

"I came out to visit you. I knew you would tell me not to, so I just came."

"You're not getting a divorce, are you?"

Carl has his lawyer's voice on and talks to me in apple country language, as if I share his references. "We are running pears at Peshastin. I am at the packinghouse all day." He pauses and his voice gets tight. "Peshastin is a town near Wenatchee where you will land." It is as if he is talking to the village idiot.

"You can rent a car at the airport," he says. "Have you learned to read a map?"

"The next plane is in four hours. I can drive," I say.

"Drive? To Wenatchee? You would get lost on your way to the Wal-Mart."

I have somehow managed to find my way through several dozen countries, I say, tracking down remote villages and dictators.

"You have people that take you around," he says. "There are no fixers in the apple country."

"I want you to put me to work."

"That's funny."

"I'm serious."

"You're going to work for seven dollars an hour? No breaks except for lunch?"

"Sure," I say.

"And don't talk to anyone on the plane. Whatever you do, don't tell people you meet that your brother has apple orchards."

18

The flight is forty minutes, and within that time I have two lengthy conversations, one with a fertilizer salesman from Spokane who is in the middle of a divorce and the other with a woman in a lavender sweatshirt who owns orchards in Orondo where she grapples with codling moth. I write Orondo in my notebook and also one of her restaurant suggestions: the Windmill. "Try the raspberry pie," she says. "The meringue is a foot high. Are you from New York?" she asks. "We are so sorry for your troubles. Were you there when the planes hit?"

From the air, the apple country unspools in front of me. Tiny flags hang on porches and the light shards coming through clouds dapple the river. I look down on what seems to be millions of trees, in all colors of the autumn harvest. I see a canopy of fruit trees, tiny apples visible from the air like a pointillist mural in crimson and gold, linked by rivers cutting through the mountains. I was right to make this trip, I tell myself. There are only a few of us crammed into the small plane. The wings bank over the top of an orchard and I can see a sign: PICK THEM

NOW. Is that an orchard? I ask, as we glide over the tops of the trees.

Our luggage is on a cart on the tarmac. It feels joyous to get out of a plane and actually walk down stairs to the ground. WELCOME TO THE APPLE CAPITAL OF THE WORLD, a small sign says on the outside of the airport. I already feel better, my mind drifting into some easier place. There is a rack of brochures on the attractions of the area—balloons, rafting, the Snake and Columbia rivers. And a small café that looks like a real place with nothing wrapped in plastic or ready-made. "The best apple shakes in America," it says. Nearby is a glass case with a T-shirt and a model of the *Miss Veedol*, the plane that completed the first nonstop flight over the Pacific.

In front of me is the orchard I have seen from the air: Riccio's Pick It Now. I am more alive than I have been in days. I am in the land of the flyover, where the panorama is of trucks loaded down with wooden crates moving up and down the hillsides. The names of the packinghouses are stamped in black—Stemilt, Orondo, Chelan. And sometimes from the tops of the bins, I see thousands of gleaming apples, the Reds and Goldens, Braeburns, Galas, Fujis, Pink Cameos, Ambrosias and Jonagolds and Winter Bananas on their way to be sorted, packed, and shipped in cargo freighters and dispatched in planes and ships to Taiwan and Montevideo, Cracow and Acapulco, Boston and Montpelier, millions of apples stamped with the trademark sticker—the red apple with the curvy "Washington State" in the middle. And the signs: APPLE VALLEY ELECTRIC. APPLE VALLEY GYMNASTICS. APPLE VALLEY CARPET. Rural America is in front of me—ten-wheelers, RV camps, fertilizer and feed stores. The women I see are in combinations of prints and plaids. Where do these people get their clothes? From my reading on the plane, I now know that the apple country has 973 varieties of fruit grown in a sixty-square-mile area—apples, pears, apricots, blueberries, cherries, dot the hillside. There are orchards everywhere, hidden behind bunga-lows, in backyards owned by secretaries and accountants. And larger tracts owned by dentists from Seattle looking for a tax break, Mormons with a history of farming in the area, agribusi-nesses like Stemilt. And you can see it all here, in these towns of Wenatchee, Yakima, Chelan, Pateros, and Cashmere. Apple juice processing plants and packinghouses, nurseries and rail-road yards. Wenatchee is a city of lawyers and burger flippers, software nerds and experts on gypsy larvae, fertilizer salesmen on the road, horticulturists with doctorates who will descend on your orchard and spend hours telling you how to prune your trees.

I drive down Mission Street and see a low redbrick building, the radio station KPQ. The *K* and *P* and *Q* are all in immense red neon apples. In the next block, the *Wenatchee World* with a golden apple globe out in front. I cross a suspension bridge over the Columbia River and see a gleaming ribbon of water that stretches to the horizon line. There is a mall with a Safeway and a Baskin-Robbins and roadside stands that advertise espresso and cappuccino. Not so bad, I think. I pass the Van Well Nursery, with which I feel like I have already developed a relationship be-cause of my airplane study of its lists of varieties.

And then there's smoke, directly in front of me, a wall of flames and a billowing cloud of black. I pull into the Baskin-Robbins. A teenage boy behind the counter seems remarkably calm, considering the smoke that fills the air. Already I can hear that I have on my reporter's voice; there's a part of me that is re-acting, there's a story here. I am not just letting this be but seeing what is around me as a sign of something deeply connected to the World Trade Center and the catastrophe in New York. I have a twinge of excitement; something new, something is going on out here that nobody knows about.

"What is going on?" I ask. He looks at me blankly. "The fire," I say. "Oh, that," he says. "They're burning an orchard. That goes on all the time. No one can make a go of it. So they sell their land off. It's no big deal."

19

I pull up to the packinghouse, nervous and unsettled by the smoke. Trucks clog the parking lot and on them are huge faded red bins of fruit. I walk without slowing down, as if I know where I am going. Suddenly, I am in a vast coliseum of fruit and more fruit, a warehouse of millions of apples and ten-wheelers and cold rooms and forklifts tucked down a narrow road just past the quaint wooden bridge that runs over a tiny brook. It takes me some moments to grasp the size of the plant. A squad of workers covers the floor, sorting, cleaning, packing, driving, hauling. Then I see him standing on a steel platform in the middle of a line of women in hairnets who are sorting the apples that are coming down a flume the size of a canal and flowing into steel baths that stretch for the length of half a football field. The roar of the machinery, thousands of rollers whirring at top speed, and water fills my ears.

At first, I do not recognize my brother. The atmosphere of mistrust and tension that I am used to is absent, and in its place is a quality I have never noticed, tenderness. Carl, a man with no children, holds an apple in his hand as if it is a newborn. All he needs to look like Mr. Rogers is the right sweater.

He wears a North Face jacket in royal blue and stands over vats of fruit, squads of apples caroming through open troughs of rushing water, the twirling apples setting off thousands of glimmers of tiny lights. The mists from the water dance in the air. There are rivers of apples bobbing, apples being whisked by rows and rows of brushes, apples coming toward me. Nearby, the rivers turn into large steel bins of water where dozens of women stand sorting and culling for size and imperfection. On the other side of the warehouse are more women, these ones wearing white cotton gloves, packing the high-end-line apples in boxes that have been size-sorted. Their hands move so fast that they're a blur.

My brother does not see me. He walks the line, watching the army of fruit being bathed, spun, and pushed along. It is now late afternoon. I have been flying all day. The war in Afghanistan is very far away.

"How was it going through the airports?" he says when I find him.

"There are National Guard troops everywhere," I say. "Even in Wenatchee. The kid here looks like he's about sixteen."

"Who would ever send a terrorist to Wenatchee?" my brother asks. Then he frowns. "Crop dusters. That's what they're worried about."

I follow him through the lunchroom and we stop to watch CNN on TV. The fourth envelope of anthrax has just been received at NBC. Paula Zahn reads the teleprompter. "No depth," he says, looking at Zahn. "Is she a friend of yours?"

We are on our way to McGlinn's, the local hamburger hamlet where everyone in town goes to eat. "Don't tell anyone you're from New York City," Carl says. "They'll get the wrong idea."

20

"It wasn't easy to get you this room," Carl said when we walked into the Hawthorn Inn. "This isn't your usual. But in the apple country no one puts on airs." The smell of chlorine mixes with overcooked eggs. The view is toward a Midas Muffler Shop and a hamburger stand called Dusty's. I carry my bags up the stairs and open the door to a neat room with apple-dotted wallpaper. The back of the motel looks out to the railroad track and the carpet store. It is an unusual place for a New Yorker to be three weeks after 9/11, I say. "Think of this as your bolt-hole," my brother says. I look at him, not understanding. "Where you can be safe," he says. "You know, when you have lost everything." Wal-Mart is across the road. I plan, I tell him lightly, to wander to Wal-Mart for an evening's entertainment and see what America is buying. Maybe I will take my notebook and do some interviews. I might get a column out of it. The mood in Wenatchee. "Suit yourself," Carl says.

"You'll ride with me in the truck tomorrow," he says. We are to drive to Cashmere, thirty minutes away down a long, peaceful valley. The local NPR station from Walla Walla will float in and out. Carl has maps and instructions prepared. "We will lose cell power when we go through the mountains," he says, as if we are in the Arctic. I hear the door to his room close. I planned to turn on the Mexican radio station and listen to mariachis, a reminder of childhood. I hardly notice the headline of the *New York Post* brought with me that very morning: "CNN Confirms Anthrax." I stare at the wallpaper with its border of tiny apples, loneliness and exhaustion suddenly overwhelming me. I want to telephone my friends, my daughter, Errie, but the time difference makes it impossible. I hear a distant train: I am as alone as I have ever been. There is no way I can share any of what I am feeling with my brother. I tell myself something will change between us if only we can both hang in.

21

And then it is four-thirty a.m. and there is a telephone call from Carl down the hall. "Wheels up in fifteen," he says. I am already on the floor with the *Body Electric*, mysteriously broadcast in what I consider to be the middle of the night. The *Morning Ministry* is on the NBC station in Wenatchee and CNN reports the fifth anthrax case. I tell Carl about it when I see him in the parking lot. He is already packing crates on the truck, his breath a cloud in front of him. The headline in the *Wenatchee World* is "Commandos' Strike Opens Ground War." At this hour, the highway is already busy. The smell of cooking grease follows us out of the driveway. What are you loading? I ask. In front of him are sheets of plastic, cardboard insulation, a tarp covering it all blowing around. "This is left over from last year," he says. "I don't like to see it go to waste." He swings himself on the truck, lithe at fifty-three, one foot at the top of the tire. I try to do the same, grunt, and fall back to the driveway.

"What happened to your Texas?" he asks. "When did you forget how to get into a pickup?" I let the remark blow by me. My brother's Texas is a collage of ranches, deer leases, quail hunts, guns, and buckshot.

Here, he says, and pulls me into the back of the truck, then busies himself packing boxes. The gesture is unexpected, not in Carl's repertoire. My brother's hand in mine.

Across the highway, a line of cars is at the espresso stand. Ten-wheelers filled with logs speed toward Canada. "There goes our forests," Carl says. "It's a tragedy. On this I agree with the enviros. But not much else." He sits in the back of the truck and sips green tea while I inhale my coffee. "You have to quit that stuff," he says. "You drink too much damn caffeine."

The Columbia River gleams ahead of us, the light from the valley igniting it. We pass the Stemilt packing empires, the size of LaGuardia. Hundreds of trucks and loading docks and an army of apple workers are fanning into the parking lot. Across the highway is a billboard with the sign AMERICAN STRENGTH! And a smiling Christopher Reeve. Soon we pass through a tunnel, and then another, the mountains of the Cascades on either side of us, the big window view and the ribbon of river cutting through it. Roadside stands advertise JUST PICKED—the Boscs, the Anjous, the Bartlett pears, Pink Ladies, Cameos, Braeburns, Galas, and Jonagolds.

"America will not buy any variety that is not a perfect red anymore. They want that tasteless, pulpy cardboard and those long toothy marks at the bottom. That's called typy. It's an apple term for those little knobs. There are so many Reds out there now the price plunged. Everyone panicked and pulled their orchards. Not me. I started planting more. You have to think out of the box if you want to survive!'

Out the window, sign after sign: FOR SALE. FOR LEASE. PRICE REDUCED. Acres of orchards with stumpy, gnarled apple trees. Now we are close to Chelan and to Lake Chelan, which stretches for fifty-five miles. The locals tout it as the Lake Como of the Northwest. "Isn't this ridiculous?" Carl says. "All of the Microsoft crowd have these places on the lake. They fly in and out on the weekends and do nothing to help the apple people." Surrounding the lake are hills of orchards, including one of Carl's, just past the Sunshine Fruit Stand. There is a menacing green sign on the fence: THE ALAMO ORCHARD COMPANY. NO TRESPASSING. VIOLATORS WILL BE PROSECUTED. And in case anyone missed the point, the same message is repeated in Spanish. How typical of Carl, I think. He stops at the mailbox at the bottom of the hill, pulls out a stack of mail and looks through it carefully, then puts it back. "Why don't you take it?" I ask. "I am checking to see if any of the employees have letters from bill collectors," he says, scowling. "You have to check on people all the time. If they are getting notices, it means they could steal from you." He slams the door on the truck and turns *Parsifal* back on.

There is an art to this apple picking. Not just anyone can do it. Carl is acting like a complete jerk this morning. He's got the Carl machinery in high gear, acting as if he is ready to scold me, to turn the blowtorch in my direction. I am to take an apple off a branch. You do it by twirling it, he says. Real gentle-like, he says. I hover on the *like*, the Texas of it. Where has this come from in his Ivy League education and law degree? The apple feels heavy in my hand. It resists my tugs, my pulling. The other apples begin to shake. The apple holds tight to his twig; it will not come into my hand. "Not so hard. These apples are delicate—they bruise easy." Each word comes out in staccato. He suddenly towers over me, the Texas accent more pronounced. "Now watch me carefully," he says. We stand in front of a line of experimental trees. The trees are thin wisps—the orchard term is "whip," the frail baby apple trees trying to get up and running, infant Pippins, Jonagolds, and Honeycrisps. "Apples are delicate," he says. "You have to twirl them, then gently pull them up—like this." The pink Honeycrisp twirls and plops easily into his hand. "Like this," he repeats, a tight smile on his face.

The wind is blowing hard. He cuts a small sliver of the new variety. Try it, he says. "You have never tasted anything like it." The Honeycrisp is both tart and sweet, and crunchy. The juice runs down my chin. In front of us are thousands of trees that cover a hillside. From where we stand, I can see the entire valley of the apple country. Two rivers flow together, the Columbia and the Methow, cutting through a valley in the foothills. It is glorious, the lines of the orchards, precise, white, clipped. Dotting the orchards are the faded red crates being filled by the pickers. How many apples can go in these boxes? I ask. The scowl returns to his face. "Bins! Not boxes. If you are going to be out here, get the language right." I stop myself from answering. Nearby, Mexicans wearing protective masks and baseball caps fill the bins with bags they had pulled from the trees. Carl hovers over the bins, picking up each apple. The scowl returns. *Esto no sirve. Esto no sirve.* The apples were flawed or marked and could not be in the bin.

Suddenly, he sees a tiny mark on an apple and begins to scream. "Someone has long nails! They are ruining my fruit." Now he is sprinting up and down the lanes: *Atención! Atención! Ven aquí!* His voice booms through the serenity of the hill, commanding the pickers to get off the ladders.

"Line up! Line up!" From a distance, I watch the crew begin to react. He looks like a lawyer on a country weekend, and then the voice, booming like George C. Scott playing Patton, the Texas rumble breaking the still of the morning. The scene unfolds in slo-mo. Men on aluminum ladders slowly turn in Carl's direction, their canvas bags loaded with fruit like a platoon of koala bears. "I better not find any long nails," he says. I back away, wanting to avoid the scene.

The row of pickers in front of him shine with nerves, don't make eye contact. Carl is now stern father. *"Dame las manos, por favor."* Show me your hands. Immediately, out fly two dozen pairs. Carl fishes through his pockets and pulls out a nail clipper, then moves down the row, handing it to anyone whose nails could prick the fruit. *Oh, I get it.* They seem okay, as if it has happened before. They have traveled from their villages in Mexico to work the crop. The same crew come to Carl's orchards every year. You can hear the sound of the clipping of all long nails as he moves through the rows. By then, Carl has mowed through his anger and is restored. "Okay. Get back to work."

I follow him down the lane of an experimental grove, the tiny wisps of trees blowing in the wind. The sign is in front of me: ESTA FILA NO PISCAR EXPERIMENTAL. Please don't touch the apples. "You have thought of everything," I say. I struggle to keep up. I ask reporter questions. I follow him through the lanes and say, *What is the yield? How many apples to the bin? What kind of leaf is this?* I am good at interviewing.

Are you kidding me? I am wild with rage.

The wind blows off the Methow River and I stuff my hands into the pockets of my fleece. Conversation has never been easy between us, so I have a list of questions prepared. I'm concerned because there've been conversations going back and forth that he and Allegra—we call her Theater Girl—want to have a baby. My first question is, Are you out of your mind? What are you thinking of? All of your energy needs to be on getting well. Is this fair to do to a child? I am prepared for him to erupt again, and he would have every right. *Your entire life you've been in a fury be-*

cause you think I hog the emotional ions in the family, I say. *Are you going to re-create that? A baby is not a King Charles Cavalier.*

On the way to meet him, I run the lines in my head. He will explode. I will hold my ground. It could make him feel young again. Yes, but then what? Who takes care of him if he needs it with an infant in the house? I have fixated on this when anyone could tell you that I have no right to weigh in on his life. What does any of this have to do with me?

I sound exactly like my mother, which is not a good thing. The alarm bell that says *stay quiet* is ringing loudly. Now I have to float the raft of the past out to sea. Family therapists call this starting the tape in a new place. I have started so many tapes in so many places I have run out of tapes.

It's a technique of willing myself into a higher and better place where the mind does not cast back to the facts of December 4, 1989, when I am in a car, hurtling down a dark street in San Antonio at midnight because my mother has died and no one has bothered to pick up the telephone—not my aunt, sister-in-law, or brother, or, for that matter, my father, making the decision that although I am around the corner what should happen is that I not be given a choice but to be told after the fact, even though I am almost forty years old. And then their reaction, as if I am the one with the problem, when I rage and am so grief-stricken that I am suddenly going seventy miles an hour in downtown San Antonio, banging on the door of the funeral home. And then saying goodbye to my mother in a setting where the room is scented with lilies, the sickening smell of the undertaker. That tape playing again and again in my mind.

Can we start the tape in a new place?

There is a short version and a long version of all of these episodes. The long version means we would have to blow the dust off every one of them, hold them up to the light, figure out who said what to whom. We can scoop up all the differences and use them as the reason to keep this going, to stay alone and untethered to each other, working ourselves into a frenzy of I Am Right and You Are Wrong. There is a certain comfort in that, a version of what we have always done, veiled over with a veneer of social grace. Or we can move forward, into the short version, searching for what linked us, flying the flag of family loyalty. I tell myself I am trying to come to view my history with Carl like the sun freckles that now dot my arms, signs of a history that has gotten me to who I am.

Anger rises like a snake. I struggle for elevation, a way out of the fear and panic and longing that attach themselves to anything that connected me to Carl. We are part of a family system in which no one can express feelings except through rage. Nothing is ever what it is. A difficulty of being a certain age is that you try to change the story line, you think about how you can get out of things or run away, and suddenly you can't. The unpredicted has become the irrevocable. The way it is.

Maybe this explains the fruit. Unlike with his family, unlike with his own life, he can duplicate, graft, then morph apples into something else again.

As always with Carl, it is difficult to read his mood. My cell phone rings and it is my friend Annie, calling from Connecticut to check in. I begin describing in full hyperbole the glories of Carl's apple orchards, the beauty of the harvest, and the complexity of growing a Honeycrisp in the Cascades. I am sounding like an instant expert, overknowing. The Honeycrisp is not just a new variety that Carl is fooling around with, but it is a marvel, although the soil conditions here in the Cascades are all wrong and it's much too stony.

I hang up and my brother flares. "You don't know what you

are talking about," he says. "The soil is not too stony, it's too sandy." Then he glares. "You may be good at reading between the lines, but you can't read the lines. You always act like you know everything." His anger is crackling, a lightning storm set off by what?

"What the hell are you doing here, anyway?" he says. "This is the apple country. You don't have any idea how complicated it is to run an orchard. You are a city person. City people think that apples are something you buy at the grocery store. You just get them in a big shiny pile for $1.99 a pound. You have no idea what goes into this thing. Growing apples is more than something that farmers do."

We walk in silence. I suddenly buzz with his rage. "You have been a prick your entire life," I say. "And whatever you do, I am not leaving. You will not send me away. You can be as angry as you want."

More silence. I am shaking inside, afraid I have made a terrible mistake and that we will be back to where we started, always in some mysterious place of no connection.

I feel his anger blow away. The molecules shift. "Okay, I appreciate that," he says.

It isn't much of a beginning, but it is the beginning. It takes me a long time to remember that almost his first words to me were *Don't bruise my fruit.*

22

. . . .

THE TRUE BEGINNING
WASHINGTON, 1945

He had Mexico in his bag of tricks. He could drop into something that sounded suave, *un hijo de México*, rolling the *r*'s just so, getting the staccato beat with the ease of a native speaker. Then, he could spin out the stories of his childhood on a ranch to include big names that she had only read about. Pancho Villa. Diego Rivera. Frida Kahlo. Revolutionary leaders, famous artists. What was he doing at a dance at the Jewish Community Center on Dupont Circle? At twenty-two, Thelma Long, working in the typing pool of a big-deal person at the OSS, the spy service of the war, was already interested in bona fides and résumés, and here he was, husky, a lieutenant colonel with a deep Texas accent, a commanding bark, an issuer of orders, tall, broad shouldered, with a canny gaze.

That night, Tommy Dorsey played. Tommy Dorsey? At the JCC? Not Tommy Dorsey, Mother later said. An imitator. Well, it sounded like Tommy Dorsey, my father said. The trombone, the long sounds, the air coming out of his mouth. They danced in a haze, did not talk much, the pull was that fast.

Blue moon
You saw me standing alone
Without a dream in my heart
Without a love of my own

It was her birthday. March 12, 1945. That night, she wore a dress of baby blue slipper satin she had borrowed from her rich cousin Franny, then hopped on the bus with the blackout curtains at her dorm in Langley, Virginia, where she lived with the other OSS girls. Somehow she had lucked into a job with the spymeisters of the war—the Office of Strategic Services—and was typing in a secretarial pool in the office of the general counsel.

Did she intuit something special was going to happen?

I saw your father and I saw my future. That was what she always said. But how much of her future did she really see?

She had, she later said, never met anyone whose sisters were on first-name terms with famous artists. And he had inside information and dazzled her with who and what he knew: the movements of the art treasures by the Allies' monuments squad to save the bombed-out remnants of Italian churches; he knew when Fala, Roosevelt's dog, was being flown in and out of battle zones.

But there was something he didn't know.

She was under a cloud at the OSS. It rocked her, the implication that she was a spy. She blamed it on another girl at the office who she was convinced had pulled the copy out of her typewriter when she was in the ladies' room. The press corps still wore spats in those days in Washington. Women were not even considered for these jobs. Inside the offices, they thought of themselves as mysterious Mata Haris, one columnist wrote, and gossiped about the former polo players, Russian princes, and dilettante detectives. They were young and enthusiastic, and a young woman with

ambition typed and studied German railroad tables, hoping to
come up with a pattern that might be useful. A directive had gone
around. "Women were biologically incapable of total objectivity."

Everyone knew that.

And that Drew Pearson, the Page Six of his day, was scum,
took calls in drugstores at pay phones and paid off the OSS typists with cash in brown paper envelopes hoping for their tips. In
1945, Pearson earned $250,000.

FDR had even called him "a liar, a lying ass."

Thelma was one of the girls assigned to go through the first
reports and letters coming from the camps.

Blurry black-and-white aerial shots, smokestacks. Impossible
to see.

What a son of a bitch, he said, when she finally told him about
Pearson, in tears.

He wanted to scoop her up, all 125 pounds of her, and take her
off to Texas, forever.

I'd like that, she said.

By the time they met, he had learned how to spin out his life
so that it sounded like a movie, his head thrown back, very Texas,
boastful and self-effacing all at once, what Texans call hilly-
billying. So he could just put it out there, that he was born right
after Halley's comet streaked across the Mexican sky in 1910, and
that he was wheeled around a plaza in Mexico in a town called
Aguascalientes. He drawled it in the South Texas way so it
sounded to her Boston ear like *awas cow yentes*, then dropped the
fact that the first memory he had was seeing Pancho Villa with his
floppy hat and braying stallion marching up and down with the
Dorado Cavalry outside his ranch. What he did not say was that
every morning his mother awakened not sure how she had gotten
from her town in the Baltic to this hellhole that packaged itself
as a paradise of spas and thermal miracles, not sure how and why

she could have married a faithless bon vivant, a spieler of stories, who sold this town as the ninth wonder of the world soon after she met him outside the Hall of Aztecs at the Chicago World's Fair of 1893. They were two kids from Kurland running from the czar and now she was suddenly called Doña Paula, and her husband, Isidor, a flirty redhead with a weakness for good cigars and Mexican girls, pumped himself up with the same honorific, even at synagogue.

Don Isidoro.

He had barely been out of Europe when he learned to speak about himself as if he were already rich, describing in detail the rabbi in Galveston, Texas, who met the German steamer at the dock wearing a white linen suit, who pointed him toward El Paso and then Chicago.

The heat worries my mother. The idea that she might be swept out of the East Coast and put down in summers where it is usually 100 degrees. By June, they are planning a wedding and he's in San Antonio for a few days writing to her, "It wouldn't be easy to keep cool anyway with what is going on between us."

June 2, 1947. She is twenty-four when Carl is born, intoxicated by the belief she has landed in "a dish of cream." She is giddy with love, adores her husband then and certainly the larger fact of his family, the owners of a chain of nurseries and a discount department store, Solo Serve. They are running patriot promotions for the war effort. She hates the heat, complains about it, misses her summers at the Cape. She misses everything—lobsters, clambakes, movie theaters that don't have colored balconies. She hates the prejudice, the day-to-day of it, the colonial atmosphere in the San Antonio of 1945. The ads for Solo Serve take up entire sections in *The San Antonio Light* and the *San Antonio Express-News*. Marrying into the Brenner family has saved her, put her on an equal footing with her brother and sister, or so she believes.

Three years later, Carl's first official welcoming act is to push me out of a window. I fly through the air, dropping from a low first-floor open screen into a soft bed of newly mowed grass. I am rushed to the emergency room to close the cut over my left eye. Welcome to the world! The family joke is that Carl gave me a gift—"a hard head." It is the opening shot, followed briskly by fists, orders, and the gaze, the Carl Look documented in family photographs. There is Carl, dutifully posed in a picture with his sister, staring off into another dimension. The screen of my memory then blanks out. It fades to black. I stare at the pictures. Try to bring this back. I am going through something that seems startling and yet has a name in the literature—sibling deidentification. Is it possible to know as a younger child where you begin without being defined by your older brother?

Here he is in 1962, a fifteen-year-old, panicky about the Cuban missile crisis. It is a tense time in America. At school, we are diving under our desks. "This is what they did to me during the Korean War," my sixth-grade teacher tells us. Get up! I want everyone to stand like this. And with that, we rise, obedient children of South Texas, and stand on one foot, our arms out to the sides. "These Commies are evil," Mr. Moore says. "Don't ever forget it." My right ankle shakes. We are there motionless for what seems like twenty minutes. Then thirty. "Know your enemy," he says. Our feet throb when we sit down and go back to the standard text on the Soviet Union.

Carl draws elaborate maps of escape routes down the Laredo Highway to be used when the Commies come. "We have to have a plan, Daddy!" he tells our father at nightly dinners. He has packed a box with supplies—tuna fish, Fritos, Cokes, bags of peanuts. A first aid kit.

The maps became more elaborate. My mother shared his nerves. "Nothing is going to happen," my father said. "This is all just propaganda. I have seen this and heard it thousands of times in the military. There will be no nuclear bombs."

"Daddy, you're crazy! I am going to be prepared. They are not going to get me," he said. He began to sleep with a pistol on the top shelf of his closet, laid out neatly next to his newly acquired collection of John Birch Society guidebooks.

Now mornings on Contour Drive begin with a volley of gunshots. Carl shooting squirrels out of the trees. Carl setting up targets in the yard. This did not go over well with the Olmos Park police. "They are sissies," Carl said. "I know what I'm doing with a gun." We live in the green zone, an Anglo enclave of bright lawns and yardmen and houses set back with leafy trees. In those houses are the *jefes* who control voting blocs and urban development, and vote Republican. On November 21, 1963, John

Kennedy's motorcade comes down Broadway, passing Alamo Heights. I am thirteen years old, caught by the photographer from the *San Antonio Express-News* in a crowd of exuberant ninth graders cheering for the president as he rides by, next to Jackie in a white dress. My madras Bermuda shorts come almost to my knees. The next morning, an announcement comes over on the PA. "The president has been shot in Dallas." The class erupts with cheers. My mother weeps on the telephone.

That was the roiling world we lived in that Kennedy was trying to calm down. Which brought him to Texas that November. Fear and anger lurked under the faces of the smiling women at the country club, there at the times when the bids for the social clubs went out and if you were Jewish, you knew that there was no chance you could be a fiesta queen. This was what David Halberstam would later call 5 p.m. segregation. At night, my father would rail against all of this. The lunch counter at his downtown store was the first to integrate. My father had to war with the Greek-American who had the concession stand. I won't serve niggers, the manager said. That night my father stayed late and instructed his warehouse crew to rip out the stools at the lunch counter. That bastard! he said. He won't serve Negroes, then nobody sits!

And that is how it remained. You stood at the Solo Serve lunch counter in the '60s to eat your tamales or BLTs.

All of these issues are debated in honors English class. We are a group with ambitions. Edith Ann Hollan, a member of the Debate Club, who goes on to become the archconservative federal judge Edith Jones on George W. Bush's short list for the Supreme Court. Lily Gonzalez, a petite Mexican American, daughter of an immigrant who did not finish high school. She is a straight-A student, always smiling, a member of every football pep squad. As the prom approaches, she is asked by a classmate from the country club set. A few weeks later she comes to our class sobbing, the only time I have seen her cry. "His mother made him break the date," she said. Years later, she ll tell me that I answered, "We need to move to New York." By then, she had moved to Short Hills, New Jersey, an enclave of WASP privilege, and was a prosecutor in the office of the Manhattan district attorney.

I have no memory of saying this to her, but it is true that my plans were already in motion. I did not share my dreams.

This was a Texas childhood, and Carl and I absorbed it in entirely different ways. The thrum of our father's hobbyhorses sucked Carl in as his anointed amanuensis. It was assumed that he was in a lockstep with his father, colonized, being programmed to take over and run the stores. On Saturdays, he was always working, watching from the office, buried in paperwork as our father walked the floor, talking to the customers in perfect Spanish, a connector of people, a solver of problems. "Let me call Aziz Shihab, the political editor at the *Express-News*," he would say. "He needs to know about this."

My father could stand for hours in the shoe department, a line of mounted trophy kills on the wall, regaling shoppers from the barrio with the tales of his adventures in Botswana, encouraging them to send their children to college. *These rich people on the North Side,* he would say, *they are trying to cheat you on education! On your taxes!* Then he would tell them that they were going to get handbills in their shopping bags encouraging them to write in to the mayor or Congressman Henry B. Gonzales, or the Texas attorney general, or the new treasurer Ann Richards, later governor of the state.

He was the people's merchant, a natural populist who thrived on controversy, reveling in his odd status as the noisy outlier. Carl and I are drilled with the story line of the Brenners, the Jewish *hacendados* of Mexico, from the moment we can talk. All those white lace dresses sent to the hills of Mexico for our grandmother Paula, who once trained to be a designer in Riga and wound up working in a Chicago sweatshop.

Religion was lost along the way.

You live in a secular world, my father said.

"Secular" was his favorite word.

Never mention religion. We are Texans. Americans. Secular.

Applying to Annapolis, my mother's brother scribbled a quick "Episcopalian" on his application, hoping he could pass.

"What's wrong with that?" my father says. "What do you think I had on my dog tags?"

"He's betrayed the family! How could he do this to Mother and Daddy?" our mother says in frequent telephone conversations with her sister, Roz, back in Great Neck.

"What is passing?" I ask at age six. I take this new verb with me to schools. *My uncle passed.* "I am so sorry," my teacher says.

In our history was the implicit understanding that religion was an idea skimmed over in a synagogue that was notable for its lack of Hebrew and deep ambivalence about all ritual. One small deli, Arnold's on Main Avenue, was the outpost of displaced New Yorkers, drawing the Sunday school crowd to pick up their orders of lox, which arrived with fanfare from New York every Friday. *Has the lox arrived from New York? Did it come?* Arnold, not long out of Brooklyn, stood behind the counter slicing fish and gave anyone from the East Coast a frisson hearing that accent in a Texas world of football and fiesta queens. My mother rolled her eyes when she stopped in to pick up an order. Arnold's arms were a bit hirsute for her snobby Boston style. "He's so *Russian*," she said softly, echoing what my friend the writer Mimi Swartz, also from San Antonio, heard from her grandmother. "There are Jews and there are Jews."

The remark was frequently repeated with less grace in my own house, starting with my father's bark: "For God's sake, they are

Russians!" The word "Russians" could apply to anyone who said *Oy vey*, had dark hair on his arms, or for that matter did not belong to Temple Beth-El, presided over by a rabbi who not only affected an accent that made him sound like Prince Charles but also sent his daughters to St. Mary's Hall, the local Episcopal day school.

The image of David Ben-Gurion holding a grapefruit in the Negev was in certain houses, but not my own. "They have no business being there! Trouble is coming! Remember I told you that," my father said on every occasion when the subject of Israel was raised.

"Milton, stop it!" my mother snapped. She was a firm believer in the new State of Israel, as she called it, running the entire description together as if it were an official name.

She was trying to come to terms with what she had seen in the photographs at the OSS, terrified by the implications, reading voraciously any and all material on the Nuremberg trials, then later watching Adolf Eichmann in the glass booth being tried in Jerusalem in 1961. Soon, my mother was carrying *The Rise and Fall of the Third Reich*, underlining it in purple pen as she waited to pick us up at car pool. She would help start a group to teach the history of the Holocaust in the local schools and did not find it at all strange that she could not tell the students anything much about the Passover seder but could reel off a dozen names of concentration camps, from Treblinka to Bergen-Belsen.

Being Jewish in the San Antonio of the 1960s meant wearing your hair like Barbra Streisand, falling asleep during High Holy Days, and making rude remarks about everything being cooler and better in New York, the promised land. At Christmas, we had trees with blue and white bulbs—"so everyone will know we are Jewish!"—and visits from cousins who were married to Presbyterians and Episcopalians. My mother served tamales made by Solo Serve employees, hams, and coffee cake with pink tinted glaze.

Yet the fact of being Jewish was frequently discussed, although the word itself was said in whispers, as if it were a condition.

Is X Jewish?

X! He's Jewish!

My mother's voice would flutter down an octave, as if the subject always needed to be mentioned sotto voce. It was the tone she used when she said *"Harvard,"* as if it were in italics. For that matter, sotto voce was supremely useful for any term that implied class, distinctions to be limned with a filigree brush. All of which makes more mysterious—and more understandable—what will happen later.

On the nonnegotiable Not Allowed list in our family were bar mitzvahs, bas mitzvahs, and membership in any Jewish high school social club. This put a definite crimp on our social lives. In Texas and throughout the South, Jewish young people traveled a circuit to meet eligibles, staging their own version of debutante balls. However secular was our family's pose, we were still expected to marry someone Jewish and, with any luck, as schizophrenic about his or her identity. One of the many Brenner family myths was that of our proud Teutonic origin. As proof of this dubious status, my father would bore everyone who raised the subject with, "My parents were educated in German! They spoke German at home!" This was said with the tone that made it seem he was a Lehman or a Schiff. These class distinctions were not to be taken lightly. We were a small community of five hundred families in a small city, and the lines were drawn as delicately as scrimshaw on a tusk.

"Guess what, Dad? You're Russian!" I told him soon after I became a reporter. "The area your family came from was under the control of the czar." He went red in the face. "We are Germans!" he said.

During hunting season, all Sundays began with our father's phone call to the rabbi. "Carl and I are shooting deer and some quail today. He will miss class." Off they would speed down Contour Drive, the station wagon filled with deer rifles in leather cases, then back in the early evening with bloody carcasses strapped to the top of the car. At the end of hunting season, my father and I had our ritual drives, cruising into the barrio of San Antonio, my father talking nonstop. Other fathers played golf or tennis or talked about Texas football. "Football is for idiots," my father said. He filled scrapbooks with the newspaper clippings of his antics—tax commissioners indicted, fraud detailed. Later, he would take on Oscar Wyatt, the scurrilous and charming oil buccaneer from Houston, whose company Coastal States controlled the energy in South Texas. The rates skyrocketed and my father knew there was fraud. For weeks, he plotted how to get Wyatt in his trap, finally offering a $10,000 reward in the local papers for anyone who knew anything. The next day, our neighbor was implicated in the scandal. "You will make us a pariah," my mother said. "I don't care," my father said. "A crook is a crook."

I later wrote about this moment. His moxie would turn out to be a blueprint for my own future, but not Carl's. His blueprint was there as well, but hidden. On Sunday afternoons, Carl and I would race through the Solo Serve nurseries, a haven of flowering shrubs, pecan trees, specimen plants of all kinds.

At the row of camellia bushes, our father would stop. "Your grandfather always wore a camellia." And then he was silent.

23

When Isidor got off the steamship in 1890, he was coming to a country that had seven thousand varieties of apples alone. Apples, Michael Pollan would later note, that resembled potatoes, that looked like peanuts, that were pulverized as soon as they came off the trees and turned into alcohol. The boll weevil had just come to Texas and would mow through the cotton crops. In Galveston, Baptist preachers blamed the Jews coming off the boats. *This flood of kikes will destroy Texas!* one said. At that moment in 1890, there were thirty-five Jewish families in San Antonio and a Jewish population of 250. In Galveston, a Mr. Goldman offered to buy every boll weevil brought to his dry goods store. He was accused of being an instrument of the devil but was later credited with helping slow the plague.

Isidor, born in a dairy town on the Baltic and a showman by nature, arrived in a country with Edison's marvels newly lighting up cities. Born in 1872, by 1920 he would watch the arrival of telephones, movies, radio, and airplanes. And with them, the mass message of apples would spread, and for the first time, huge numbers of trees would be sold throughout the West. He rode the trains and in

St. Louis noted the sidecar of Jay Gould at the railway station. Inside, the bankers vanished in a haze of blue cigar smoke, their white camellias on their lapels. *If I ever get rich enough, I will wear a camellia.*

History in the Short Form:
Soon after 1900, Isidor is in Mexico, scrambling for a fortune, the first of five he will make and lose and make again. He is calling himself Don Isidoro, trilling the *oro*, allowing others to take their hat off to him and refer to him as Doño. Again the *n*, written with a tilde, trilled just so, rolled, strung out. Don Isidoro has a short man's swagger. He knows how to push the aura, to package himself a winner, and bend everyone to his will. He knows to follow the money, and the money is in Mexico, ripping off the peasants, stripping the silver out of the mines on their lands, sending it back to the United States in railroad cars. The smelting industry in Aguascalientes made the Guggenheim family of New York the cash that would finance museums (those ramps!) and, later, the high-flown antics of Peggy in Venice.

Isidor promoted himself as a sharp trader, preening that he was from Kurland, a duchy on the Baltic run by the czarina for her German relatives, a shtetl with a German accent. At all times, he carried with him a German flag. He wore one on his lapel. Those who displeased him were exiled from the family, forced to beg to be reinstated.

Two daughters and two sons were born on the ranch, and for the first years of his childhood our father, the baby, was doted on by his mother and his older sisters, with the firstborn, Henry, in boarding school in Mexico City. Soon, Mexico is consumed by revolution that will kill more than a million people from 1910 to 1920 and take back the vast landholdings of foreign powers. In Aguascalientes, troops of Pancho Villa and the Dorado Cavalry camp outside the ranch. Isidor is asked to help out running medical supplies for Villa; Paula makes wedding cakes for the Villistas taking brides. As Americans are murdered in Aguascalientes, the family is spared.

Soldaderas tend to wounded soldiers outside our father's window. As a toddler, he watches the thick-jawed gaze of Villa. Anita later described it: "The famous Dorado Cavalry galloped past, and the infantry kicked up the dust, and the Indians stalked solemnly by, and there was an airplane too, that sputtered and roared and circled miraculously in the skies."

At the age of four, our father was in his mother's arms watching his father sell everything to get out of Mexico—his piano, Anita's circus pony, Paula's favorite dresses. Isidor's German flag waved from his carriage. Inside a picnic basket, gold coins were smuggled in the orange marmalade.

The Brenners were on their way to San Antonio with little but their immigrants' nerve. On the train, Don Isidoro has an idea: a clerkless store.

And something else: *New Creations in Fruits and Flowers* by Luther Burbank. Isidor had it with him in Mexico and marked the frontispiece: "Keep this Catalogue for Reference. You Will Need It When These Fruits and Flowers Become Standards of Excellence."

He had checked a Japanese quince called Dazzle and a French prune offered for $3,000 by his new business partner, Clarence Stark.

"We Are Now Standing at the Gateway of Scientific Knowledge," Burbank wrote.

You have made this up, Carl says.

Our grandfather finds a space to rent in a deserted building that was once a county jail. It's a time in San Antonio when there are separate doors for Mexicans, who are shunned at the schools. The Brenners are called "little greasers" at the synagogue. One of Isidor's first bold moves is to decide that he will hire Mexicans, encourage their business, and re-create what he had in Aguascalientes.

SOLO SERVE, THE CLERKLESS STORE.

Headlines in special advertising sections trumpeted Isidor's flair for promotion.

> FREE SAMPLES AT FOOD SHOW STARTING FRIDAY
> Aviation coffee served from a special booth; tasty cakes at the Brown Crackers and Candy company booth; Mexican foods at Gebhardt Chili Powder; pumpernickel bread from the booth of New York bakery, coffee at the H&H coffee booth, and special treats at Pioneer Flower Mills.
> CARNATIONS FREE TO LADIES
> FREE BALLOONS GIVEN TO KIDDIES
> BOOK SECTION NEW SOLO SERVE FEATURE
> STORE MADE LARGER, COMPLETELY CHANGED
> QUALITY LIQUORS AT THE LOWEST PRICES OF ALL TIMES
> Calvert's Club—98 cents
> Imported Vermouth Cinzano—79 cents

I try to imagine Anita, a zaftig Jewish girl, back in Mexico just a few years later, pushing her way into the studio of the photographer Edward Weston. "Take my picture," she said.

He was hungover; it was rainy. He made notes in his daybook about the skies of the bluest blues, the rain-washed streets, the golden silences of the capital's early morning hours. He had a leonine profile with small chiseled features and the vainglorious expression of a man who loved to seduce women. He was masterful at getting them to pose nude for the camera, homing in on the tiny hairs of their bellies, the curves of their breasts and thighs.

He was, by all accounts, a cad, but women adored him and flocked to his Mexico City rooms.

His particular fetish, it turned out, was for lissome bohemian Jewish girls. Bodies, like snakes, uncurled for his camera. He doted on the svelte form of his sultry Italian photographer mistress, Tina Modotti. There she is, laid out in full fantasy, the thick pubic hair, the legs spread. And Miriam Lerner, lean with a dark mound, shown in recline, a Jewish Venus, her skin without a pore, ready for Weston to devour.

On Anita, he had no such designs, but it is clear she would not be turned away.

"I reluctantly prepared my cameras," he wrote in his journal after she left.

Turn around and bend over, he told her.

And suddenly, or so he later wrote, he saw it: the pear.

The forms came to him like great spheres of white blankness, porcelain plains. The light was dim and he saw, for the first time in his life, abstraction, what is possible to create.

He noted in his daybook: "Yesterday I 'created' the finest series of nudes I have ever done and in no exalted state of mind. I was shaving when A. came, hardly expecting her. . . . I made excuses, having no desire—no 'inspiration' to work. I dragged out my shaving, hinting that the light was poor, that she would shiver in the unheated room. But she took no hints. . . . And then appeared to me the most exquisite lines, forms, volumes. And I worked easily, rapidly, surely."

The next day, he studied the negatives with increasing astonishment. "They retain their importance as my finest set of nudes— that is, in their approach to aesthetically stimulating form."

The photograph was a masterpiece, widely acknowledged to have changed twentieth-century photography.

They called themselves "the family," this group of Anita's

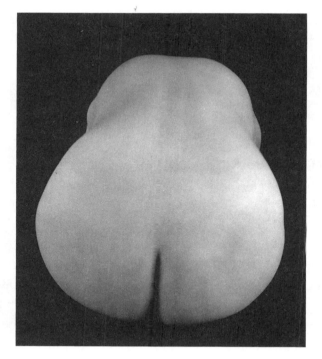

friends: the painters Diego Rivera, Frida Kahlo, and José Clemente Orozco; Weston and Tina Modotti. "I am a Fucking Wonder," Frida wrote on a sign on her backside, mugging for Anita's camera at a party in the '30s. They both were.

Anita introduced the Mexican muralists to a New York audience, bringing Diego Rivera and Frida Kahlo to the city, promoting the work of Orozco. *Idols Behind Altars*, illustrated by Edward Weston's photographs, made the front page of *The New York Times Book Review*. Anita was at parties with Sergei Eisenstein, was doted on by Lionel Trilling.

She rode a comet for a decade, then gradually faded.

I make notes on these backstories, still convinced that they are significant.

24

Gerry has only one piece of her premium coconut pie left. The regulars know she makes it twice a week and rarely advertises it. Tonight the blinking neon sign outside says RASPBERRY PIE. And GOD BLESS OUR TROOPS. Gerry's system is famous in Wenatchee. She starts taking reservations at nine a.m. Gerry answers the rotary phone on the wall by the counter and then prongs the piece of chocolate pie or marionberry or lemon meringue with a toothpick. No names are ever taken. Tonight, Gerry's flavors are chocolate cream, lemon meringue, chess, raspberry, marionberry, and apple.

I'm at the Windmill early. The *Wenatchee World* and the *Times* are spread out in front of me and I am trying to hear CNN coming from the kitchen. Almost every piece of pie has been speared. She is closing out the last of the raspberry meringue. "I'm having a fight with table fifty-six. They say they called special to reserve the coconut," she says. There's a group of us who share space at the counter. It is October 10, the bombs drop on Kabul, and Bush is out there with a statement: "Now is the time to draw the line in the sand against the evil ones," he says.

"Take the chocolate cream with the candle to the table in the back," Gerry says. I recognize the blonde in a mauve sweatshirt from Mitzy's, a hairdresser at the Wenatchee Valley Mall next to the new Bon's department store.

"You know it's over when your husband tells you how much he hates *The Golden Girls*," a woman selling Clinique said at Bon's.

The pies are lined up and I fixate on the raspberry with its mile-high meringue. I am suddenly making notes on the tongue-and-groove wood on the counter. "You ask a lot of questions," Gerry says. I order a salad, dressing on the side. "We'll do the best we can," she says, a shadow falling over her face.

"We have to bomb the hell out of them," Carl says when he joins me at the counter. Wenatchee has gone to war. The crop dusters are on high alert. Hastings Books had a sign that read GOD BLESS AMERICA. By the time the bombs were flying over Afghanistan, True Value had up its own sign: PRAY FOR OUR SONS.

There's a newspaper in front of him and a ballpoint in his hand. He's circling stories on the op-ed page. He's focused on an editorial about gun control. "Anyone who thinks they can take our guns away does not understand this country. Our Constitution. Our ideology," he says, scowling at me as if I am what he hates, a card-carrying, flag-burning evangelist from the American Civil Liberties Union. He uses their initials as shorthand to underscore our divide. "You and your ACLU friends in New York don't understand how the people in this country think. You live in some kind of elitist bubble there. The president is a great man. He is a leader. He knows we have to take on these terrorists and we have to win. America cannot be attacked. It is our moral responsibility to go in there and show these Arabs a thing or two. We have to bomb the hell out of them."

My New York life has melted away.

Carl looks at me, then blows past the entire subject. This is what I hate about the men around me. Conversations exist on two planes that cross a galaxy and never connect. Suddenly, he pulls out a book and lays it on the counter.

"What do you know about the Shasta daisy?" Carl asks. He has with him another biography of Luther Burbank from the Wenatchee Library and makes careful notes on the father of horticulture on a legal pad.

"Burbank is responsible for everything in modern fruit growing," Carl says, as I strain to listen to the news from Kabul.

"No one in America knows who the hell Luther Burbank is anymore. The fact is that he was as famous as Henry Ford. He was photographed with Thomas Edison. He figured out *everything* there was to know about plants. How to graft. How to breed. How to do it *all*. They think he's a town in Los Angeles."

He is suddenly vibrating, causing Gerry to look over from the cooler. "Would you like another coffee?"

Then, as always with my brother, a fast where-is-this-coming-from change of tone. "You are on the floor tomorrow. I need you at the packinghouse. You have to make sure my pears are going to go out without a bruise."

I am half listening, making plans in my head somehow to get to Kabul and be in the first wave to report on the Taliban and the liberation of the women. Thousands of blue ghosts throwing off the burkas and twenty years of camouflage. Who could I arrange a fixer with?

Carl looks at me blankly, eyes lolling back, drifting away. In the best of times, he is incapable of sustaining a conversation that is not about himself. I have to trick him into paying attention to me by saying, "Carl, this will interest you." Now he snorts at the Windmill. "Yeah, right. *Vanity Fair* is going to send you. Sure. And you'll wear a Kevlar vest. You'll be there with the rockets flying. Where will you get your hair done? I don't think there are any beauty parlors in Kabul."

25

A single step, four months earlier.

I meet him at Victoria Station. We are tentative with each other, still. He wants to go to the wedding of a close friend's niece in Sussex, in the English countryside. A band, a buffet, a group of friends. His current love, Theater Girl, has rehearsals in the States and cannot get away. I want to get through the rivers of anger that divide us. *I will be in Europe,* I lie. *I'll meet you there.* *Great,* he says, with what sounds like genuine enthusiasm. I borrow a cartwheel black straw hat and pack a short black and white dress, a pink feathered evening bag. *Buy him a tie,* my friend Deeda tells me. *He will love that.*

I'm going to buy you a tie, I tell Carl. He's astonished. Why would you do that? he asks. Because it's fun, I say. Let's go pick one out. We walk through the tourists of Buckingham Palace in time to see the changing of the guard. I lived in London in my twenties so it's a kind of coming home for me.

From time to time, Carl would come to visit. At the time of one of these visits, I had fallen hard for the boozy bureau chief of *The New York Times.* He was known for his fluency with prose, could tap out a flawless five thousand words in a few drunk hours, and had, among his other war stories, the moment when he told Bobby Kennedy that Martin Luther King had been assassinated. He had also predicted the nomination of Georgia governor Jimmy Carter as the 1976 presidential candidate and was not shy about letting all of this drop within seconds of meeting any woman under the age of thirty. "I am going to marry you," he said the night we met. "Let's call your mother right now." My mother greeted my wacky passion with a telegram, "Beware! 40 plus newspaperman is NOT marriage minded."

On our first night out with my brother, my beau, as Carl called him, looked into my brother's face and said, "I have not written about Giovanni di Paolo in some time. I need to think again about Renaissance Siena." His face was mottled with tiny red capillaries of late nights and war zones. His eyes disappeared into his cheeks.

"Is that so?" Carl said.

I was still in my ex-pat phase and making notes in my diary about London life. A standard question at dinners: *Have you seen the new Fragonard?*

Later, Carl said, "Why are you with that guy? He drinks way too much."

Now it is June, twenty-four years later, and we dance to a band that sounds like the Four Tops. Have I ever danced with Carl before? He's met me at my hotel just off Kensington Gardens. The flowers and wreaths for Princess Diana's death four years earlier continue to pile up at the gates of Kensington Palace. I've been meeting in New York with a new set of doctors. "If you do not take a mass of chemo when you get back, you will not be here in a year," I tell Carl. Bikers and walkers race by us on the Hyde Park flower mall.

Goddamn it, he says. *I won't do it.*

After the wedding, he's on his way to Paris for a weekend. I hug him at Victoria Station and see a tiny church a few blocks away. Something draws me in. It's a Sunday, and the priest is about to read a passage from the New Testament. The theme is "Remission." They are still using the King James version, High Anglican style, reading before communion: the classic liturgy about blood and bread and the body of Christ, and what can happen in remission after you repent your sins. All that weekend, it is what I nag my brother about. He is trying to enjoy himself, using the swing dance routines he's practiced to doo-wop and drinking champagne. I have to stop myself from saying, Please, get the damn chemo, you will get a remission. A remission.

I am not making this up.

The simplest gesture could undo me. The sign that there was a fissure in Carl's outer shell.

The next thing that happens is that Carl says to me, "You are on the floor."

I am set to work the fruit run, the days at the packinghouse where the big red bins get delivered to the warehouses, hauled and bathed and cleaned and sorted. I'm working the belt with a woman named Blanca. We wear white paper shower caps and place bowling-ball pears into Panta-Paks. It's an awkward fit because of the size of the pears. Blanca has been working the line for a decade and comes from Oaxaca, a town in southern Mexico known for its carnivals on the Day of the Dead. Each November, for two days, the bakeries are filled with sugar skeletons and skulls made of puff pastry. On the holiday, families take picnic baskets to the graves and play loud mariachi music to celebrate.

Blanca grows cherries and prize nectarines in her yard. We carry stacks of boxes marked "CMA Cooperative"—these will be packed and shipped around the world. The pears will come hurtling down the flumes, revolve on racks, be examined for quality and size, then get dried and sorted. This is the process of getting the fruit off the tree and into the store. Although Blanca has been packing fruit for a decade, Carl wants, as he said, "family eyes" to make sure that his pears will be packed down and shipped absolutely flat.

A woman named Darcy is on my other side. "Were you there when the towers fell?" she asks me. "Do you think you could find me a key ring with the towers on it? I want to remember them."

Carl moves down the packing line, coming toward us, his face cut with tension. For all he knows, these pears will come back once they are opened. He worries about the black spots. "Your brother is a control freak," Darcy says.

The view out the window is of snow peaks. I am as far away from my world as it is possible to get.

"You want to do something?" Carl says.

He walks me back to Darcy's station, then pats each box. It is necessary that the plastic is smooth. I copy him, gently tapping on the bumps. "Careful," he says sharply. It takes hours, and from a distance, I see Carl walk the lines, inspecting every box. Tension radiates around him.

The pallets of fruit are stacked on the forklifts. I've learned a new term: fruit run. They count them at the packinghouse: four thousand five hundred.

I've fallen into the routine. Carl takes me out to the Cashmere farm to pick boxes of apples from the experimental trees. When I get there, Sadot, the farm manager, has Shiny, the blond orchard dog, sitting on the front seat of the truck. A damp wind blows and the empty orchard boxes fly out of the tarp. I watch Sadot and Carl try to tie them down. Carl radiates purpose and goodwill. I think about the grower Grady Auvil, who brought the

Granny Smith apple to Washington State. At ninety-one, he was still breeding new varieties. "I don't have much time left to do everything I need to do," he said. He paid for the rent of his employees at the Auvil orchards, channeling almost all the money he made back to the people who worked with him.

I follow Carl back down the highway, marvel at the architecture of the tarped empty fruit boxes and the elaborate rope ties that he has engineered.

I think of all the wasted time.

I'm on the floor, sorting through all of the plastic sheets, and placing them in the empty apple boxes that I am taping up. Each box is to hold five hundred Panta-Paks. They have to be counted perfectly, Carl says, suddenly irritated again. I close my eyes and hear my father's voice. The decency underneath the gruffness, the code that you had to read.

There are hundreds of Panta-Paks in front of me. Pink and purple and green. Each one has a number for the size fruit it holds—#9, #12, #15, #17. A wallop of fatigue is coming on. I've got a Walkman in my jacket and tune in to a press conference with the president. He wants, he says, to put America "on notice." I sit on the concrete floor of the warehouse with a notebook by my side, making stick figures, diagonals to show groups of five.

"You have to be exactly precise," Carl says. "I resell them. If you make a mistake, it gets expensive." They sell for pennies.

This is the kind of trait that drives me crazy about my brother. All these fussy details of plastic sheets and smallness as his life rushes by. And is my life any better? Will I look back and say, I wish I could have reported on more sugar lawyers?

"China is already selling its juice extract to Tree Top, and all their apples have killed the export market in Washington State," Carl says.

How can Carl save his farm? What can he do to put himself ahead? How can he market the Asian pear? I have a list of ideas in front of me—specialty vinegars to be sold for $15 a bottle at Whole Foods. A *poire* from Washington State we could market for cognac prices? How can he come up with a niche that could make these apple orchards work?

I'm working with a felt-tip marking pen, labeling the boxes with the color-coded Panta-Paks. Suddenly, the top rolls away, underneath a bleacher row of seats. I don't see it. I am fifty-one years old and I panic. Carl will be angry about this. How will I explain this away? I have a daughter in college and a writing career, and I am worried about a pen top? The afternoon is now colored by this fact, and I crawl on the cold concrete trying to get it, fail.

"What are you doing?" Carl says, when he walks into my corner of the warehouse.

"I lost the pen top to the Sharpie," I say.

"So what? It's only a pen top. For God's sake."

After a few days, I forget I have another life. We have no history here.

"Check this out," I tell Carl. "This is pathetic. We are a generation that seeks wisdom from the sides of tea boxes."

"What are you talking about?" Carl says, pushing a grocery cart in front of me.

We are making our daily visit to Fred Meyer One Stop Shopping, a stadium of food just over the suspension bridge in Wenatchee that links downtown to the road to the airport. The supermarket is one of those coliseums of supersized everything, kept arctic-cold even in late October, when it is already chilly in the Cascades.

I stand in front of a display of herbal teas and have in my hand a celadon green box from the Tazo tea company of Portland, which is fighting for market share with Celestial Seasonings.

"Listen to this," I say, following him down the aisle. "'Tazo / Tah-Zoe / noun, the act of being transported to a place of past memory by a specific smell.' Like a madeleine . . . Get it?"

"Did you get the cantaloupe?" Carl says, ignoring me.

"Yes," I say.

He rummages in my cart, pulls a melon out of the plastic bag, and feels the stem. "This isn't any good. It's not ripe."

"Smell it," I say. "That's what Mother always did."

"I don't remember that."

I push the melon into his face. "All those trips to the *mercado* when the melon farmers would come up from Uvalde and set up on their trucks? Hello?"

"Oh, yeah."

"And all those stupid coupons she used to carry?"

"What is wrong with coupons?" He suddenly opens his brief-case and pulls out a folder with dozens of tiny cutouts for coupon specials. Tide. Bounty. Poland Spring bottled water. "You can save a lot."

"You spend more on gas coming here every day than the coupons will save you."

"That's ridiculous," Carl says, angry. "Let me see the tea box."

I watch him read the other side of the box:

"'When the spirit of a village started to fall and people lost their enthusiasm for life, the leader would often summon a tea shaman to distribute Tazo, which gave the community a renewed sense of joy.'

"I wish we could figure out something like this to sell my apples," Carl says. "Those damn hippies are so clever."

———

The stars are out in the parking lot. I am suddenly filled with joy that we are here together, two only children in the same family, trying to connect.

I take a pose, the Tree I from my yoga tape. *Check this out,* I tell Carl, putting my foot on my upper thigh and striking the fierce look of concentration called *drishti,* the gaze on a fixed object in space that gives you a sense of peace.

"Is this a new New York thing, Marie?" Carl asks. "You do that on the Upper East Side?"

Patience.

"You have to mirror everything he says," my friend Paula, a Boston psychologist, advises me frequently. Paula has a twin sister and a personality of purest empathy, but more than that, she helped guide her own husband, the love of her life, through thirteen extra years when he was struck with cancer before he was fifty. I know Paula because she is the sister-in-law of a dear friend. The circle of love in these women surrounds me, and through these adopted sisters I struggle to learn a better way to be. Paula finds me researchers, clinical trials, and a doctor in Palm Beach who will give Carl an experimental drug that he has read about. Her sister-in-law Lesley suggests doctors from Staten Island to Boston who might be able to help. All of them bombard me with calls and much-needed advice. We are women in a crisis, guiding each other through.

"This is about affirmation. About making your brother feel loved and supported at all times. Try saying this: 'You.' YOU YOU YOU. Do not use the word 'I'—someone who needs as much support as your brother cannot hear the word 'I.' Now do what I say. 'You.'"

I hang up and try it, the words catching in my throat: YOU YOU YOU YOU YOU YOU YOU YOU YOU YOU YOU.

Soon after, I learn about the late psychologist Carl Rogers, a guru of affirmation and person-based therapy. Rogers had two big words he used to describe personality: "congruent" and "incongruent." Congruent people were just fine—somewhat like Saint Francis of Assisi, sailing along in the sea of life without the need for anyone to kiss their ass or to make them feel okay about themselves. Incongruent personalities were all the rest of us, who keep peeking under the toadstools for someone to tell them how cool they are and who could, in extreme circumstances, wither and blow away if they felt unseen. It has to do with a need to feel pumped up like a balloon. If you had a full-blown case of the incongruent virus, you could deflate at the tiniest blip on your screen, doing a version of "poor me." *Poor me. Poor me. Poor me.* For years, Carl and I tossed our own football of neediness and incongruencies back and forth, passing each other in the field.

27

We are in the doctor's office at a small medical building down-town. You are silent, always silent, but push at me a copy of your medical report.

Adenocarcinoma. "Mr. Brenner is not a smoker but had smoke damage from his military training."

Is that how it happened?

After all that tough-guy posturing in college, you never got to the marines. You enrolled in the National Guard in the same champagne unit that George Bush wound up in and spent the next three years in law school. We were together again on the campus at the University of Texas. You were filled with lightness. You had learned to fly a small plane and took girlfriends on rides through the hill country, flying low over the trees. "This is God's country," you said, which surprised them. One of your girl-friends told me this much later.

How are you just sitting here? You have your leather attaché case and cell phone and you look as if *you* are the doctor, that nothing in the world is wrong. You are using that same silver Cross pen you keep neatly on your dresser. Soon the cell phone will ring. "Let's go over the orchard plan for tomorrow, Marc," you say briskly, as if you are sitting at your desk in the shed. In front of you are cards and numbers and clipboards. You have a typed sheet, a lawyer's sheet, a sheet with the stats. Now you are always annoyed. Annoyed at filling out the charts, annoyed at the waits in the offices, annoyed that you are asked one more time to recite the history of the case.

Dr. David Spiegel has written studies on connectedness. His theory, in brief, is: You can cure cancer if you are connected, if you are in someone's life, if you are there with him or her all the time.

It's weird to see you like this. You look just like you did when you ran track, still muscular and lean. I make notes in my notebook of the history of the case. The "light chemo" you have soon after your first surgery in Houston.

You tell Dr. Nott about your blood counts, the whites, the good cells, the history of your CEA. "I cannot believe you look as well as you do," Dr. Nott says. "No one would ever imagine that you were in anything less than tip-top shape."

You beam.

On the way out, I squeeze your hand. "Don't hang the balloons yet," Carl says.

I see that he has my Spiegel studies in his attaché case. This pleases me. It does not mean that he will read them, but it makes me happy just to know that he put them there.

Everyone hates an expert. You cannot cure anything, much less cancer, with connectedness. What you can do is pretend you are doing something by pushing stories through a fax machine, spending hours on the Web looking at clinical trials. You can say "Andrew Weil" and "integrative medicine" and "Let's go to China" and "Does anyone know anyone who knows the lung man at Duke?"

You can call and write and speak and fax the MRI.

You tell me not to fax so much, that someone will read the faxes, that someone will know the score.

I don't want anyone knowing anything, you say. And that includes Casey and everyone you know in San Antonio and most of the people in New York.

I have already told everyone I know.

You fax me the following: a list of Chinese herbs—Chinese yam, atractylodes, licorice root, Chinese date, white peony root, red peony root, drynaria rhizome, astragalus, codonopsis root, glehnia root, schisandra root, cornus, poria, tangerine peel, cinnamon twig, coix, ginger, bur-reed rhizome, zedoary rhizome, bugleweed, frankincense, myrrh, Szechuan lovage root, salvia root, vaccaria seeds, corydalis rhizome, trichosanthes fruit, pinellia rhizome, hedyotis, scutellaria, selaginella.

You say: I am going to China. I don't trust anyone to treat me here.

I am convinced at this moment that my level of interest in the apple world is sending a message to Carl, filling up the mysterious divide between us. If I can ask him so many questions, we will be able to fill in all our silences. I keep promising myself I will learn to listen, to not talk so much, to not have to tell what I know, but this is not really working.

Silence is the beauty secret of the over-fifty set. Let's all be honest about this. What they say when women of a certain age take up more than eleven seconds of talk time is, she must be lonely. She's lonely. Lonely. She's a woman alone, out there, having to talk so much. It's a power strategy, to pull in, put on sunglasses and appear to be the Sphinx. I want to practice this. Saying *umm* or *let me think about that* when someone asks me something. To not tell stories that have Texas at the heart of them, but to keep it to the short form—the CliffsNotes version.

"You would last three hours," my daughter told me when I announced I would spend the next weeks in an ashram taking a vow of silence.

"You're not listening," Carl says.

I *am* listening, but I am finishing my morning yoga, working on the exercise where you say you will put your ego aside, stay in a healing mode for the other. I struggle with these lessons, the bad girl of the yoga shalas, still confused why it seems that 99 percent of yoga teachers I have ever encountered are bossy and have problems with their own egos and continue to burn scented candles and incense when their students ask them not to.

I am also, at the moment, trying to stand on my head, not so easy when you are no longer a size 4.

"It seems to me that you are always with someone who is completely disconnected," I say, "who is not on your side. Maybe that's why none of these women make you happy in the end."

Something I have skittered over: Carl is always surrounded by women.

You are going to have a ticket dispenser with numbers like they have at Zabar's for the motel door, I tell my brother. *All these women flocking here.*

Is that a joke?

It's raining when the Breck Girl arrives. It is probably unfair of me, but I secretly name them. I have just missed my personal favorite, Allegra, this slim beauty we call Theater Girl, who had to rush with her wheelie bag to get back for rehearsals when the next wheelie bag comes down the hall.

Breck Girl has arrived late, almost at midnight. She is here perhaps to make a Hail Mary pass, to try to get Carl away. I have no proof of this, just a younger-sister feeling. This gets more interesting and surprising, I tell Ernie on the telephone. *You are missing everything.*

How can anyone look this good at five a.m.? There she is, a cheerful wisp in impeccable cashmere, each blond hair in place, her voice a drift of Texas meringue. Her voice floats through the pear trees. She has a symphony of questions. *How many pears in those bins? What is the yield on each tree? Have you seen how they trellis the fruit on the Amalfi coast? Lemons and oranges all in tiny nets and they make it much more productive?*

What is it that you call this orange blush on the fruit?

I watch Carl open up like nightshade. He's suddenly got one of those huge Asian pears in his hand and is showing her a tiny fingernail. "If there is more than this big a mark we do not ship them!"

She's brilliant at playing to him, a Southern diva who knows how to attract men. She homes in on him with the big brights on high beam. First, the adoring look, the laminate stare. Heather has the confident manner of a woman who had been doted on by her father. She is a talker, a nonstop flatterer, the eyelashes down, like Princess Di.

"I get so dizzy in the mountains," she says, clinging to his arm. I follow them as Carl holds forth on the cultivation of the Cameo. I have my camera with me. "I don't have one good picture of me with Carl," she says, stopping every few moments behind a tree, laden with ripe Asian pears. She poses with the pears in her hands, as if they were shining baubles ready for display.

"All these shiners!" Heather says. "You should make apple brandy! Or sell apple jam."

"Right," Carl says.

I feel a big wave of muteness coming on. I know that I am getting into that younger sister mode, somewhere between jealous and more jealous. Heather is a certain kind of Texan, a woman who wears a size 2 and it is all just so, what a decorator calls matchy-matchy and warns you never to do. So the tweed jacket is just the shade of the cashmere sweater, which is tucked into the pants. She's chosen to bring leather pants and a shawl from Loro Piana, the cost of which would sustain some of these farmers through the harvest season.

Heather's ex-husband had a nickname: Tres. That's something you hear in Texas in ranch families who have a son with a III after his name. Tres is the number 3 in Spanish, a South Texas family name. In their last trip as a couple, Tres and Heather did a Boone and Crockett circuit.

"What is that?" I ask.

"Antlers," she said.

"Antlers?"

"The biggest, the best, the showpieces. You know, a six-foot spread on an elk. A fifty-six-point deer display."

Heather says, "So Tres and I were in Wyoming going from trailer to trailer trying to hear how these hunters got their trophies! They watched and watched as the deer moved through the mountain and they just waited. And now these antlers are going for $100,000 in Mexico and twice that to the Saudis who advertise for them on the Internet."

This conversation cheers Carl up and puts him into the zone

of normal, his normal. To his credit, he would not dream of buying a Boone and Crockett anything, even if he could afford it, or, for that matter, a Chola bronze. He's way too cheap.

At breakfast, waiting for Heather, he tells our waitress. "I would like to substitute a bran muffin for the fruit."

"That will be extra, sir."

"It shouldn't be. The fruit is more expensive."

"That's our policy, sir."

He stares her down.

And then we are on the sloping hillside of the Cashmere orchard, the Columbia River winding just below. Carl has planted the pears down a row of white wooden trellises that stand like sentries in a grove.

"Wouldn't this be the greatest place for a wedding?" Heather says. "Imagine the bride and the groom coming through this pathway, the arches all decorated with grapes and apples. All of their friends watching them and clapping. Wouldn't it be fantastic?"

The fruit was now at full tilt, the sun gleaming off the Columbia River beneath us. We stood in front of the very trellises that were on the cover of *Good Fruit*. Actually, it did look like a perfect place for a wedding. The white wooden poles leaned together like a long aisle, the brushed orchard grass soft under the feet.

Carl was silent, staring at Heather. He had that look, somewhere between panic and love.

We are to meet at the packinghouse. Heather has a map and that look, like *I am in charge*. As focused as a GSM. "It's just a mile or so away," I say. "No real need for that."

"Carl said you could get us lost. He says you have no sense of direction," she says. "You know how he is. I don't want to get him upset. I do everything he says."

Then: "We have always been in love with each other. But the

timing was never right. . . ." She stares out the window toward the mountains. "I should have brought him my tarte tatin. Why didn't I think of that?"

There is no sign of Carl when we drive up Dryden Road toward the Peshastin Pinnacles State Park and his orchard. I park the car by the shed and walk across the road to wait for him to arrive and sit on the fence in front of Sadot's house. Sadot comes from Oaxaca and is, Carl believes, the best apple man in the valley. Carl takes him hunting and has taught him new pruning methods. I watch Heather look past him out into the hills.

"These orchards are a financial disaster, aren't they?" Heather says suddenly. "I bet they don't make anything. I know a lot about farms and ranches. You can never get any cash out. I bet Carl has lost so much money here."

Well, you had to give it to her. She was putting it right out there, even to the sister. She had grown up on a South Texas ranch and been in charge of her younger brothers and sisters from the time she was twelve. Unlike the other women from San Antonio, Heather was a cold-water rinse on a chilly day.

"I always have been in love with Carl," she says again, suddenly teary. "What am I to do?"

That night, she wore the leather pants to Cuc Tran, the local Vietnamese café, where you could not spend more than $22.87 on dinner for two. It's a hole in the wall right in the center of town. Wrapped around her is the $1,000 shawl with all the rusty paisley leaves swimming in the pattern.

Soon after, he calls me. "What are you doing?"

I could hear the desk chair in the shed.

"I need you to come over to the Cashmere orchard right now."

"I'm in the gym," I say. "What's up?"

"Why don't you take Heather on a long drive so I can get some work done?" he says.

When I arrive, I see them out walking through the trees and race to catch up with them. Carl looks relieved.

"Let me show you something," he says.

Soon we are climbing through the Galas, up through the Bartletts, the valley stretched out before us. We're standing in a row of saplings, just planted in this sandy loam soil that he has named after our father.

The Milton bloc.

"This is where I want my ashes scattered," he says. "Are you listening to me?"

Suddenly, I cannot stop crying. Heather remains dry-eyed. "We will see to it," she says, without missing a beat.

29

Time unspools. It takes forty-eight hours for the Breck Girl to leave the orchards, with him kissing her good-bye, calling her *darlin'*, and promising her he'll be back in San Antonio just before Thanksgiving and that he'll stop by and have her special pumpkin soup the night before. I make it without cream! she says. Just a little chicken stock and the rest is pureed pumpkin! He's handled it all well, deftly, with no one getting hurt feelings and no harsh words.

We're going along fine, talking about Silverio, his favorite picker, who knows how to manipulate the ladders in the orchards. He has me race to OfficeMax to make up more signs for the pickers' houses. He puts up a grid of rules for the crew: NO BEER! NO WOMEN IN THE SHED! PUT THE TOOLS AWAY AT NIGHT! He is worried about the bins, that the pickers will not monitor them, will not take proper care of his fruit. He knows that after they have worked apples, they will pack their boom boxes and their hoodies and move south, looking to harvest nectarines.

We are in the truck, loaded with Galas, headed for the Pateros farm. Suddenly, the dark sounds of Smetana fill the air. Carl pulls over to a cappuccino stand. *When you plan the memorial service, I want Smetana,* he says. *I want his* Má Vlast. *My Country. Are you listening to me?*

This is ridiculous, I say. *You are not dying. Dying people do not eat two desserts. You are up every morning at four, running up and down these hills like an athlete.* But he was right. I was spinning. Sometimes all that is required is the ability to listen.

At night, I go to the movies and come back to see him in the lobby, staring in the blue light of the computer screen, the swirl of clinical trials dancing in front of him. *Adenocarcinoma.* The survival rate is 11 percent. We're all dying, I say, when he quotes this number to me. It's just a question of when. Or I say, "I don't believe in numbers. Numbers are just numbers. They do not mean anything." I continue on as I have been.

I am trying to climb into my brother's head. It's a weird place to be. Each time I think I am onto something, some new labyrinth opens up. How can anyone truly be interested in the history of the apple?

It is a crazy idea to patent an apple. Everyone understood that in 1893. I am now operating under a theory, a leap of logic, that has not one shred of fact as its basis, Carl points out to me constantly. I am stuck with an image that plays over and over in my mind: Isidor Brenner, at twenty-four, on a train, trying to sleep on a wood bench, moving from El Paso to Chicago, hoping to work a job at the World's Fair. He has with him the *Jewish Farmer* and a sheaf of papers of land grants and jobs that might or might not be available.

And then our grandfather opens his eyes and sees the trees.

You can't just make this stuff up. You have to stick to the facts, Carl says immediately.

Your mind is so damn linear, I say.

But underneath, I see that he is listening, taking it all in.

In *The Botany of Desire*, Michael Pollan has written extensively of the nineteenth century and the sweeping apple craze in America. For Pollan, the apple was a history of rags-to-riches fables of fruit growers—"a bright metaphor for the American dream." Apples, Pollan noted, hyped hometowns and home states with patriotic pride—Westfield Seek-No-Further, York Imperial, Rhode Island Greening—and the inventors themselves: Norton's Melon, Moyer's Prize, Payne's Late Keeper. Americans flocked to fruit fairs in Philadelphia and New York. Growing apples was considered glamorous and romantic, a fad that swept America like the Fletcher diet, which demanded chewing every bite thirty-two times. It was a time of spirit tables and cider orchards, apples raised to go right to moonshine.

The apple was frontier sugar, an instant high, a drug to set off a war of apple polemics between Mr. Nature, the wild-eyed self-styled guru John Chapman, known as Johnny Appleseed to generations of American children, and the Stark family, the first titans of apple agribusiness, who tried to control market share. As Johnny Appleseed traveled down the Ohio River on his way to schoolbooks and Disney movies, he pushed his nature-is-holy philosophy, dropping seeds for trees and crusading against the evils of grafted apple trees. The Johnny Appleseed philosophy was right out of the Ralph Waldo Emerson playbook. Apple defenders swarmed the Starks, yelling about the assault on the noble seed.

Chapman was pushing his own brand hard, with nurseries that reached from Pennsylvania to Indiana, Pollan noted—a "barefoot crank" wearing a coffee sack when he died but leaving twelve hundred acres of prime real estate. He brought "the gift of alcohol" to the frontier.

The fact was this: The Starks were the Carnegies of fruit.

This is a no-brainer, I tell Carl.

I have a brochure from the Stark Brothers Orchard with me in Wenatchee. I bring it to dinner one night and watch Carl look at it, say that's interesting, flip through pages of engravings of fruit fairs on the Mississippi. Then he turns back to the *Wall Street Journal.*

I hope you are buying gold, he says.

You better get the hell out of the stock market. There is going to be a collapse. These money managers steal from you. You are going to lose everything.

I am already an expert here, reading out the facts of the history of fruit, the business of fruit. I am now sure, I tell him, that the myth of Johnny Appleseed, a nineteenth-century hippie working the farms with his seedlings, had superseded a family of fruit pioneers who were truly original and mostly unknown in the history of the apple.

Their names were Clarence and Edgar Stark. The two brothers with their silvery hair had built up the first big commercial nurseries in America, bombing the Midwest with vast plantings, putting their slogan on barns: STARK TREES BEAR FRUIT.

I read him a quote by Ralph Waldo Emerson e-mailed to me by my friend Dick, an Emerson scholar. "The apple was an 'incarnation of thought.'"

"How about this?" I ask. "'The globe on which we ride is only a larger apple falling from a larger tree.'"

"I am trying to read," Carl says.

We had come to a place of parallel play where we could sit at a table and have what we call reading dinners, so we could be together, yet neither of us demanding blood from the other, just allowing each other to be in his or her zone of silence.

Suddenly, Carl asks, "Do you and Ernie have intimacy?"

"Carl! What do you mean? Do we have sex?"

I never know how to answer that question. Something like, "Of course, we are married." Or, "Of course not, we are married."

Carl turns bright red. "What I mean is, do you talk?"

"Yes," I said quickly, not wanting to let him in. "We talk all the time. About everything."

Carl turned away, a shadow over his face. I could look into his eyes and see a moment, then a cloud of loneliness behind it, as if he wanted to take the conversation further.

I moved away and started again to read out loud from the Stark brochure.

"It is all here," I say. "Grafted trees were available as early as 1801 and were already controversial. A fight erupted about this—the grafted tree lobby warred with those who favored apple-seeds."

I had lost him. When I looked up, he was buried in the monetary tables.

What interested me in the Stark brothers was not the Wikipedia fact load I was dumping on my brother but something else.

Yes, the Starks were the pioneers of industrial agriculture. Yes, their business model was unique—they put their trees out for propagation and understood, in the best case, that that process could take seven to ten years. It was a time in America where the cities were lit, Thomas Edison's marvels were at fairs, the telegraph linked the world and here, Eureka. I tell Carl: Try this. It cannot be a coincidence that Isidor took this in on his way to Chicago, determined to get a job at the World's Fair of 1893.

It has to be true, I tell Carl. *You can figure this out. This is why he becomes the King of Nurseries. You cannot not say this is completely amazing. It is where you got it, the apple thing.*

I wasn't slowing down for a second.

Isidor knows about the Black Way and the White Way and the pavilions of Muslim Hall. There's an exhibition of Aztecs and Mayas and the Nursery Hall of Wonders, with exotic plantings that no one has seen. He is determined to be there, six hundred acres and pavilions touting the new.

This is what he knows, coming to America, just off the boat.

America is cowboys and baseball.

And something else: apples.

And just then, the first nursery monopoly spreads from Missouri to Washington State. Stark trees are shipped on trains from farm to farm, but they are losing market share.

Stark Trees Bear Fruit.

I was unsure where to take all of this, but the theory took hold of me. I was stitching facts out of what I learned, trying to come up with a grid to lock together all of the following events. There are certain unfortunate people in the world who feel they have to solve the riddle. At this moment, I was one of them. Where was the pattern? How did it link?

"It doesn't connect," Carl said. "It is complete bullshit."

Somewhere near the Shenandoah, Isidor gets off the train and bikes through Iowa, where he is hired to be a clerk at a local store. As it happens, he is not far from the town of Peru, the farm of Jesse Hiatt, the future orchardist of the Delicious apple. He reads and hears and hears and reads about fruit fairs, the marvels of Luther Burbank. Isidor sells Stark Trees. America is a farm economy and Luther Burbank the rural Einstein. Webster's had a verb in its dictionary, "to Burbank." It meant the hybrid breeding of plants, much discussed by Darwin. For decades, Burbank was known as "the wizard of horticulture" and the "genius of gardening," determined to record scientifically, as Mendel had earlier, all the results of his plant experiments. He used the word "hybridizer" and started the study of what became genetically engineered fruits and plants.

Burbank was attacked from the pulpits of America shortly before the Dreyfus case in France: "How dare he interfere with the handiwork of God?" He introduced eight hundred varieties of plants, and later thousands of hybrids, 113 different plums. All of this was foreshadowed in an instant bestseller, *New Creations.*

At that time in America, the Starks struggle to retain their hold on the apple world. The Panic of 1893 devastates their company and they turn to what they are good at—fruit promotion. They blanket the West with promotions for a fruit fair. It is called for Louisiana, Missouri, where Mark Twain once worked as an apprentice.

Isidor keeps a black ledger notebook. Okay, I made this up. But he could have put a label on the front: New Ideas. In it, the following:

1. Shredded wheat—cereal in a box, introduced at Chicago World's Fair

2. A pancake mix that is eggs and water

3. "When You Plant a Stark Tree, you can depend on it."

Consider the ironies in this.

How do you know this didn't happen? I ask Carl.

I still believe, or want to, that I can view a scene in one way, culling what I am absolutely convinced at the moment is the essence of what is wrong and has always been wrong, or what works, and then I can spiel it out and he will see it just the way I do. Because of course I am right.

Marie, you are so right.

Why didn't I ever think of this?

I cannot tell you how much your sweeping generalizations, judgments of people who lived fifty years ago, and ability to connect a mass of unconnected material fascinate me, especially now, as I am thinking about whether the clinical trial that is being offered at Columbia Presbyterian is going to save my life.

Underneath our conversations, I know I am fending off something, dancing too much, talking too much, hoping that something I say will cause the door to unlock, to keep Carl closer to me. And keep him alive. The past is powerful, the beginning of everything.

Carl is facing the endgame and I am running.

I always run.

Sometimes to live, you have to dart away.

There is nothing wrong with this. ADD is the necessary survival strategy of a certain age.

As Carl struggles, I am there and not there, with him like a shadow on a screen.

30

Carl and I have a date to meet at Prey's Fruit Barn to check out all the new varieties. I drive past rolling hills, candy cane orchards, fighting for space on 97 with the ten-wheelers on their way to Canada. I am getting zooey in Wenatchee, so far away from anything familiar. Twirling the dial, all I can get is prayer radio on four channels and the orchardist report. The sky is dark with rolling clouds, and thunder causes me to jump in my seat.

We are unaccustomed to being together. I have my costume on, asking him questions, not allowing any stillness to be in the air. It's hard to know where he ends and I begin. I have a journal with me in Wenatchee, and I am finding it hard to use the word "I."

He's standing over a plastic bin of sample apples when I drive into Prey's. The wooden Indian out in front has a list of all the varieties—Mutsu, Haralson, Mollies Delicious, Red Fuji, Valstar, Wealthy, Liberty, Idared, Ginger Gold. The list covers the board.

Carl eats twelve apples a day. There's something holy about the way he twirls the skin off the fruit with a hushed respect, watching the peel as it becomes longer and longer, one strand, one perfect strand. Today at lunch he's been hearing two growers talk about trying to pull out their apples to cultivate a new crop, the Zing cherry, somewhere close to a Bing but heartier and redder. There's talk of it going into Oregon, it's playing big in Europe, and the growers are thinking that the high prices for soft fruit, as they call it, are going to save their land.

There's nothing Carl likes more than sitting at the Anjou Bakery, talking about the Zing and asking Sofia for a tiny wedge of the huckleberry pie, or a single handmade chocolate, or some of her crunchy new biscotti, fresh out of the oven, the pistachio nuts cracking in our teeth. Carl relaxes, the strain comes off his face, and he lists what he would like for dinner, the fresh-grilled salmon at Horan's. He caught it himself in Alaska and froze it. There are fiddlehead ferns at the farmers' market, morels too, he says. We'll get her to sauté them in the best olive oil—and not too much.

We stare at the pie. I stab another berry, taste the crust, and a good calm wave comes between us. It feels somehow lucky to be with him, the barriers of a lifetime beginning to drift away. I am suddenly in awe of my brother, seeing him for the first time as a person who made himself part of an entirely unknown world. At the next table, two women in faded T-shirts are talking about a Dutch Romantic concerto they have heard in Yakima, the Bose sound that is in the halls. Suddenly, Carl is very un-Carl-like; he's in their conversation, talking about Bose sound and how you can hear every cello, every string. "Have you ever heard Clair de Lune on Bose?" he asks. The wind riffles the baskets of purple and white petunias that are on the front porch of the Anjou. We're just there, quiet, watching the trucks move up and down the highway toward Bob's Fruit Mart. Behind us you can feel the breeze coming off the river.

"I'm glad you're here," he says, suddenly, then looks away.

31

A fast-forward in time.

From: Apple Man / Alamo@applecountry.com
We are picking Fujis and have finished the pass we are making
through the Braeburns in Pateros. We will only be picking the
Fujis tomorrow. We should finish this pass through the Fujis on
Saturday. We will then pick up the rest of the Braeburns in
Pateros on Monday and Wednesday. We will clean up all the
rest by next Thursday. The weather should cooperate. It is
cooling down, but not freezing. Last year at this time we had a
severe cold snap that came through that froze the fruit on the tree
for a week. It caused us to send the Braeburns remaining to
Treetop for processing for juice and the Fujis got sent in also. All
told we had 150 bins that were froze and sent to Treetop. The
weather looks more favorable this time around.

I am making tapes. I am making tapes because that is what I
do: interview people, turn on a tape recorder, check to make sure
that it is running, ask them questions, then later, much later, or

never, take the tapes—the hours of testimony—and type them, transcribe them, listening to the voices alone in my office with the trees of New York outside my window, changing season as the voices surround me, Indian accents and Washington lawyers and women in trouble in the Bronx and France. I listen for patterns and inflections, hear "facts," and figure out the shape of a story from some offhand remark. I try to craft the complexities, take the scenes, push them together in a way that makes sense for the magazine I write for. "It is . . ." "According to . . ." "It never occurred to . . ." I am making a tape on Friday, October 7, 2005, realizing that I have come back to the apple capital of the world because making tapes is how I survive. It is the way I reach for "distance," confirm that I am "a witness." I am outside the event although I am in the middle of it. It is protection, part of the latex that covers me. Making tapes allows me to reprocess, to craft a grid that I can understand on situations that are incomprehensible.

At this moment, I suddenly want to change everything that is me, the observer part, and move into something else: the living-your-life part. When does that start, exactly? And something else. I look into the mirror and someone says: *What are you doing here? You have no right to live.*

32

Does it matter how he heard the news?

2001: Carl is in a crop duster, flying low. With him is a drafts-man and a photographer, charting each and every one of his trees. If he can calculate where the sun falls and at what time, he can enhance his fruit, prevent the orchard burn that happens on the sides of the Goldens. The soft Golden apples bake on the tree, turn brown and then to mush. Every year he loses thousands of apples to sun heat. The sky is bright blue. Next to him is a photographer who has taken this assignment. He is to photograph 100,000 trees in three orchards. "No one has ever asked me to do anything like this before," he says. Acres of trees planted in neat rows, the carpet of them, vast, green, and dotted with fruit that they can see as they fly low. Carl is desperate in the small plane, waiting for a call, waiting to hear what he does not want to know. He hides it, as he always does, with a frenzy of motion, as if the completing of the ordinary tasks will somehow keep the facts away. In his pocket is a pen and a paper. "When you have differ-ent bloom timing," he tells the photographer, "it is important to understand how the sun falls." He planted northeast to southwest,

APPLES AND ORANGES · 147

understanding that the south side of the tree is always warmer, causing the Goldens to turn.

In front of him, Lake Chelan. His horizon is all water, all trees. At this early hour, the lake is glass. He sees on the lakefront markings where developers are planning places called Clos CheValle and Hawks Meadows. Already, the apple trees are pulled out, and there are signs that houses are coming in. There's talk of vineyards and the land management acts—Controlled Growth and Growth Management.

Later that day, he will drive six hours to Walla Walla and check in to the Marcus Whitman Hotel. It's a redbrick pile with a Klondike Trail charm near the good restaurants favored by the locals from Whitman College. Carl wants to take a look at Washington's Napa—the vineyards near Walla Walla—then drive the loop deep into the southern Cascades. That's the future, those vast corporate orchards run by Stemilt and Zirkle Fruit. We don't have a chance, Marc, he says. You have to stay ahead. This is what he does, drives like a maniac through the highways of the Cascades, as if there is a purpose to it, not just what it is, a way to not be in his mind at that moment. He can listen to his books on tape—David McCullough's *Truman* is his new one—after he gets done with the new Robert Caro Lyndon Johnson biography. The voices calm him and also the idea that he is out of the swamp of self, hearing about the greatness of another life.

He comes back from these short trips reborn, as if everything is new. The term he uses to describe the miles and miles of corporate trees in the southern Cascades is: "the lunar landscape." At the side of the road there are walls of apple crates that read CHIEF WENATCHEE. The cold-storage rooms are the size of Penn Station. How can we compete with that? His friend Denny Evans cries at breakfast, telling him, The banks are trying to foreclose. You can't make it here if you have less than a thousand acres of working trees. Denny, you have to be forward-looking, Carl tells him. That's what Truman believed.

And then, the call. *Carl Brenner?*

I thought it might be something like that.

He was suddenly in a frenzy and called Marc. "Could you send me the orchard plan for the day?" his voice catching. He gets up with the cordless phone and walks back into the office to consider the tree plans that are spewing out of his fax. It is a system that he has designed, each and every tree labeled and coded: "G" for Gala, "B" for Braeburn, "F" for Fuji, and all of it stamped with "GM" for the Gala Milton bloc, the patch that he named for our father. Carl showed him soon after he came to Washington. Often he spent hours just looking at the yards of plans, laid out on a long drafting table, 110,000 trees, each one diagrammed, noted, marked.

He makes a decision. He will not make a phone call but will write it all out in a letter. He works on it for hours, reworks it, retypes it, checks for spelling and details, reads it to his friend and confidant George, a banker in Baltimore. George and Carl were close in college and have been constant allies in each other's life. "I am going to tell Marie in a letter," he tells George. Then he drives to the FedEx office and carefully fills out the form. "I don't want it there any sooner," he says, checking a box that will ensure it arrives on the Monday after Thanksgiving weekend. "Are you sure that is a good idea?" George asks. "It is the way I am doing it," he says. "What is the point after all of a lot of conversation? When did it ever change anything? You know how she is."

So he stays alone in the apple country and spends his time making a list of everything he needs to understand.

The list starts with a single name: Luther Burbank.

He drives to the library and asks for a biography of Burbank. He has so much to understand. If he could re-create the experiments of Burbank, understand what first went into grafting, what Thomas Jefferson had understood about the apple, the cultivation of some moldy species called the Bellflower, then he could divert himself from the larger story, the cells that are moving in on his organs, dancing through his body. If he can think about what Burbank did a century ago, then that would answer everything.

33

Excuse me, but I think I talk too much. I can tell by the way you look at me that I have irritated you with my manner. I am too New York, too city girl, but really, what can you see in it out here? Today I have with me a list of fruit terms that I will ask you about in the truck. I have this list because, to be frank, I am struggling for conversational topics. What is "bitter pit," and what is "apple scab"? This is what I pretend I want to know.

You look at me with that look and clench your teeth. Bitter pit is when fruit has a stain in it, you say. And apple scab is something that happens on the surface of the fruit. And then you say, But you really do not have to know all of this.

3 4

. . . .

I have six months, he said. *If I don't find something, I'll be dead.*
Tears streamed down his cheeks.
Help me.

The swamp comes with me in my suitcase to Wenatchee. As I
grind away about the past, Carl is relentlessly going forward, re-
sisting all my attempts to replay my version of the family tapes. I
could close my eyes and be in the room the day our mother died,
see his face over me, cut with anger: *You should have been here.* It
was two a.m. I was around the corner and got a telephone call.
When I arrived moments later, she was gone, her bed stripped.
My aunt, sister-in-law, brother, and father sat in a room. "We
thought it was better this way. You would make a scene," Carl
said. I screamed, "How could you have done this to me?" My
aunt held up the telephone so her husband could hear me breaking down. Her face had a sly expression, a "gotcha!" For days, she
had sat by her sister's bed, trying to make up for lost time. I would
walk into the room, wanting to be alone with my mother, and she

would say, *You can join me.* Then she would give me a look if I left to be with my friends, wanting to be on my own.

"I can't do anything about it," my father told me one day in the kitchen. "This is what happens between siblings. Everyone tries to make everything right in the last days." My aunt overheard and stormed out of the room.

Two days later, my mother died. My heart was broken. I was two weeks away from my fortieth birthday and could not imagine a life without her, the North Star. I rushed to her bed to see the sheets stripped one hour later. *Why didn't you call me?* I screamed. *I went back to the apartment to be with Casey. I was five minutes away!*

I screamed at my brother: *You never do the right thing.*

I screamed at my aunt: *How could you have let this happen?*

Everyone grieves in their own way, she said coldly. *This isn't going to bring her back.*

Then I rushed out of the house, speeding in the middle of the night to the Roy Akers Funeral Chapel on Main Avenue, passing the San Antonio Public Library, banging on the door, howling that I had to be let in. It was balmy that December, and the San Antonio streets were deserted. I watched the signs flash for La Fonda, the Mexican restaurant on Main Avenue that has not changed since the days of Harry Truman. Across the street, the library glowed in the moonlight. *You're going to die young if you don't do something, get some help—something,* our mother told Carl a few days before she slipped into a coma. He was tense with her, angry that she wanted to fire a nurse. We had turned her airy bedroom into a hospital suite. *I don't like her,* Mother said. *She gives me the creeps. I have too much to do to deal with all of this,* Carl said. Her face had drawn over her bone structure, but her essence remained. *You can't go through your life like this,* she said, almost her final words to her son. Carl stormed out of the room. A few minutes later, the telephone rang. My sister-in-law was with her. "Thelma, it is someone asking for Mr. Brenner," she said. "I divorced him years ago," Mother said. My sister-in-law later reported that there was no sense that Mother was making a joke. *Probably the morphine,* Carl said.

This was a period of life that would never be spoken of again. It couldn't be, if we were to move on. We had been coded with operating instructions: Push through life with a sprightly performer's brio. Don't let a dark scenario cloud your vision, except in late-night wanderings through the house. Sleepless hours that were never discussed, never explained. We learned to skate around the edges of larger questions. Was there anything wrong with that?

"You won't see me this morning," I tell my brother. "I'm off to research the history of the apple."

My voice has pushed up a few registers, as if I have gone through a nether zone.

PRESS ME, reads the red button at the apple museum. The apple museum is on Mission Street, down the road from *Wenatchee World*. It's a dank hall with gallery displays of a century of Wenatchee Apple Queens. In front of me are dioramas of the Wenatchee territory when it was a stop on the Klondike Trail. Two women with silver hair and skin as thin as lace sit at the front desk, a basket of giveaway apples in front of them. "Could you tell me where the display is for the largest apple pie in the world?" I ask. I had seen the picture—the apple pie the size of a sidecar that made the *Guinness Book of World Records*—and assumed that the pie was kept here, as frozen as Mao in his tomb.

The women look at me blankly. I repeat my question and they begin to laugh. "That pie was eaten years ago!" one said. "We just have the picture from the newspaper."

Now I am on my way to the basement, passing displays of farm equipment, single-engine biplanes, and rusty tools—the Wenatchee version of the Smithsonian. Suddenly I am alone in a gallery in front of the button: PRESS THIS TO LEARN ABOUT THE APPLE.

A video display and a farmer in overalls who sounds like Tiny Tim. "Today in Winterset, Iowa, there is a six-thousand-pound stone commemorating the original red apple tree."

It celebrates Jesse Hiatt, a man with long hair like a stoner's, who cultivates his chance seedling, pushing it out of the earth, repeating it for years, until he gets the perfect apple: the knobs at the bottom, the color a vivid scarlet with white stripes. It is as sweet as chocolate, unusual for an American apple, the sugar brought on by the intensity of the sun in the Iowa orchard. The tree grows and grows, up to twenty feet, producing an apple that Hiatt will call the Hawkeye. Hiatt has hopes for his monster red.

At the display case, I see my reflection in the glass. My façade of cheerful reasonableness, ginned up after many readings of self-help books, has eroded, and I am ready to explode.

I have a notebook with me and am struck by the dates. 1892? 1893? Isidor Brenner was in the area then, trying to absorb everything he could about the New World.

A fact has emerged from the Brenner archive, a fact wholly unknown to Carl and me. In Aguascalientes, Isidor had an orchard. He spent his days grafting limbs onto trees. There is no doubt in my mind that he had with him a catalog called *New Creations*, the bestselling monograph of Luther Burbank, the Edison of trees. He will, throughout his life, introduce countless rare varieties of plants to Texas, showcased at Solo Serve. This fact will be noted in his obituary, but was never mentioned in our house.

I spend days at the motel attempting to lay out the case. By now I have read all the letters between the Brenner siblings. Mudballs hurl back and forth between them:

You have no right to judge my life.

You have not called your own mother who has done so much for you.

Dada is very satisfied with his young genius son—who gets a by-line once a week while the sob sister on the paper gets ten. Pero no lloro. *I don't cry.*

I present them all to Carl, with pastel Post-its marking significant passages. There is no doubt about it, I say, you have inherited your love of fruit from a phantom, a crazy redhead from the Baltic whom we never knew. *What bullshit,* Carl says. *Throw those letters away. Who cares about this stuff?*

35

I'm late to meet Denny Evans. Carl is trying to get rid of me this morning and has cajoled Denny into giving me a quick horticulture lesson on the pear. He's got his armor plate on again. The fixed smile, the stiffness, the sign that he is under attack. It is all there, as if he is a different person, trussed up for battle with my brother—the real brother I saw in the packinghouse when I first arrived, now locked away in some other place. Hey you, what happened to that man I saw who picked up an apple like a newborn? What happened to that other, better you, the real you?

I'm taking my time to get there. I know that Denny will be out on top of a mountain somewhere and that his son Guy will have to look for him on a cell phone that he won't answer. So I will get to taste Guy's new homemade chèvre at the fruit stand and pretend that I haven't already eaten three apples today. Guy is fooling around with Pinova, a variety that is battling to get out of the experimental fields in Chelan. You can spend hours there, tasting and driving up orchard lanes, looking between the trees.

Denny is waiting for me. I follow him up a hill behind the farm stand. He stops in front of a gnarled pear tree, bent to the ground. "'You plant pears for your heirs.' That's what they always say. You can't kill off a pear tree no matter how hard you try. They are indomitable. This one is about your brother's age. As gnarly as he is, too."

Everyone is in slo-mo in a farm town. This morning, at the A&P, I was trying to pay for my *Wall Street Journal*. I put the dollar bill down on the counter and got stuck behind one of those farm women who look like a sidecar from behind, a supersized fortress of muscle. She was taking her sweet time checking out the vacuum cleaner bag display near the only glass door that lets you out. "Excuse me," I said. She turned and looked at me, then said, "I guess you're in a hurry today." I wasn't especially, but she was picking up my aura. It is clear that I am a weird alien from another world, about as out of my depth as it is possible to get.

"Guy has been spending too much time in Seattle with the granola people," his father says. He is cranky this morning, fed up with Guy's marketing ideas.

I've walked into a family conflict. Denny, in tears, has met Guy at the train station. For years his family has grown apples in the area and he has put two sons through college on the income. One son is a trader for Deutsche Bank in New York. Guy has been to film school. Denny has ninety-five acres, and he will lose it all if the banks will not restructure his debt.

Guy has come back to Chelan to try to help Denny save his orchards. Guy is tall and lanky, with dreamy eyes. He wears Carhartt overalls, the faded homeboy clothes of farm kids. He's a child-man of thirty, but he has come up with a plan— "sustainable farming," he calls it. Rotate crops and go into the fruit version of "food with a face." It's in its early days, and almost no one has heard of it. Guy hands me a copy of a paper by a farm philosopher based at Iowa State University. I look at the title: "The Small Farm Movement."

"What does this mean?" I ask Guy.

"Going broke," his father says.

Denny is urbane, doing well, living on the water in Lake Chelan, on first-name terms with the apple kings and the packinghouse tycoons of apple agribusiness. For months, Denny and Carl planned how they could rig a buyout of part of the Dole orchard plant.

Then life changed.

It came fast and hard. Denny couldn't meet his payments, and the banks called his loans. He was suddenly in his fifties and without a future, without funds.

A panic has hit Washington State, and you can hear it in the conversation of the growers. They meet in the mornings at the Apple Cup Café. How are they going to hold back the billions of apples being grown in China, produced for pennies by a trillion Chinese? This question gnaws at Carl and at Denny, whose orchard borders Carl's in Chelan. Denny has now leased part of his trees so he will not be forced to sell. Do you have to try to buy a share in a packinghouse to compete with agribusiness? How could the small farmer survive in a global world?

I am carrying my tape recorder and notebook in the car.

Carl and Denny now debated the wisdom of the Honeycrisp. Could anything save their orchards?

By the spring of 2001, Carl had made the decision. He would consider planting the Honeycrisps. He knew, he told Marc and Denny, that there were problems. He listed them on a yellow legal pad. Later, I will find his notes in the Orchard box:

1. The apples that grew were very large with a tendency toward bitter pit.

2. Stem splitting

3. Thin skins

4. Growers were reporting a pack-out rate of 50%.

He was focused on what he wanted to achieve. A normal pack-out rate—the apples that could actually be used from the trees—was close to 80 percent, but the delicate nature of the Honeycrisp was a challenge. Still, it was selling for three times what any other apple brought. Carl worried about the quality of Honeycrisp that was coming from his row of experimental trees in Pateros. Pateros was warmer than Chelan without the cool breezes of the lake. The Honeycrisps were often mottled, but Carl was hopeful for Chelan. Denny was onto another idea, graft some limbs of Ginger Gold to the Honeycrisps. At night, they compared the statistics coming from the Michigan apple orchards. They spoke on the telephone, Carl in Texas or in Washington, Denny on his cordless phone looking at the lake. *I think we are taking a risk here*, Carl said.

Opinions were sought from experts, the fruit scholars of another age.

I am making lists, buying tapes at Staples, trying to understand the crisis in the orchards.

Every time there is a dip in the apple country, reporters from Seattle find Don Heinicke for a folksy sound bite about what's happening to the farmers. He's a local celebrity nicknamed King of the Reds, the man to see in the Central Washington Valley, a

bluff Oklahoman, a talky historian of fruit varieties in a place where most of the farmers are mute.

In 1977, Heinicke strolled through a friend's orchards to check out his crop. He noticed one flaming apple glimmering on a branch. It just called to me! he said. "It had a light around it. The way it was striped! The toothy quality at the bottom. It just looked perfect."

Heinicke glowed. "So what did I do? I stayed quiet. That was the first step." He would have to return to the orchard and try to cut a limb to see if it could reproduce. He had the secret thrill of discovery at a time in the apple country where the Columbia basin, fifty miles away, had yet to be planted by agribusiness.

He continued his walk with his friend. "Do you mind if I come back and take some cuttings?"

Four years later, that cutting became the Red Chief. It was a mutation that had just appeared. The same way that a Granny

Smith had just appeared on a tree in Australia. Soon Heinicke had the buds on a row of experimental trees. He filed a patent for the Red Chief. More than a million trees were sold by the nursery that developed it, and the grower cashed in: $1 a tree.

It was a bonanza in apple terms, and American grocery buyers had a brief flurry with it. Redder than the Delicious, with a superb and tangy taste! Then the moment passed. The Red Chief, however, made Heinicke famous in the apple valley. It was the Red Chief and all the hundreds of varieties that explained why everyone tried to hang in now that times were bad.

"Well, now, just forget it. You pay two thousand dollars an acre to plant a variety of apple called the Jazz. Crazy stuff! You have to buy the trees and then plant them, but you don't own the trees. The people who have the patent do!" Heinicke laughed one of those isn't-that-just-so-damn-ridiculous laughs. "A New Zealander owns those trees!"

"You remind me of your brother," Heinicke says. "All those questions. You even ask questions in the same way, just getting right to the point."

3 6

· ·

From: Apple Man / Alamo@applecountry.com
Things continue to progress here on the farm. We are getting
thinning done in a timely fashion. We are thinning the Goldens
in Pateros and will start the Goldens in Cashmere Monday. The
labor situation for us has been great, and we had a good crew
come in and stay with us. This has not been the norm for the
growers around us. Many Help Wanted signs appearing. The
crop looks good and we will try to stay away from the hard white
things that fall from the sky.

All for now.
Marc

The noise from the ten-wheelers is particularly loud this morning. It must be the direction of the wind or the sound of trucks
filled with logs that have been cut in the prime Washington forest
lands. You see the trucks coming down the highway with thousands of trees, trees to make paper towels and papers and all of
the waste in America and the world. They rock on their ten-
wheelers, the forests stripped.

The Columbia River stretches before us. The days are now routine. I am in Carl World. Here is how it goes: five a.m., late to start farm day at harvest. Out to the fields with the pickers, packing apple boxes for shipping around the country, monitoring the fruit runs at the packinghouse, checking on orders going out through the cooperatives and to the fruit buyers who have been cajoled into buying Carl's Asian pears. Then trips to Wal-Mart, six p.m. dinners in town with the local growers. The sun begins to break through the clouds as I drive by Lake Chelan. The mountains shimmer off the water and all the bleakness disappears from the day. The tightness in my stomach begins to fade. I am starting to understand what has brought Carl here. I've driven the loop, circling by the cutoff for Spokane and Okanogan, driving straight through the mountains toward the Anjou Bakery.

"You're not bored here?" Carl asks as we ride in the truck.

"No," I say quickly. I know not to say to him what I believe, what I now have convinced myself to believe. That if I can keep him in my gaze, nothing bad will happen. At Anjou, he's circling a catalog. He reads out a trip he wants to take: the Alaska big-salmon fishing trip. "'Fly into remote snow country in the summer and fish the big fish . . .'" he reads.

"I am taking that trip, no matter what," he says.

I get out of the truck and say, "By the way, I'm looking for a little house to rent in San Antonio."

"You would do that?"

"Yes," I say. "You know my theory."

"Yeah. The healer gets healed." His face darkens with contempt.

37

The plan is hatched almost by accident at Central Market in San Antonio. Carl stands in front of a pile of Asian pears, his favorite Arirangs with an elaborate sign painted by the produce manager: MEET THE GROWER.

Central Market has become a travel draw for Southwestern foodies who fly in and out of San Antonio to marvel at the lush spread of specimen plums and white asparagus, lobsters the size of tennis rackets, and islands of pizzas and picante sauces, cheeses from thirty nations on display. "This is a reason to move back here from New York," my friend Naomi tells me. "Destination shopping!" Cooking lessons and demos and masseuses and boutique growers and ranchers who set up special booths where the Alamo Heights crowd samples their wares.

When I find Carl, he's slicing pears for a crowd, juice dripping down his hands. "I'm busy right now, but we need to talk," he says brusquely. He stands in a fuchsia polo shirt, thinner than he has been in weeks.

I wait for him at the café. Allegra has flown in for the week and is assisting him in the booth, looking confused and delighted at her new role of pear queen. I've noticed she's using the word "we" a lot to describe the harvest. "We had such a tough time with the Chelan bloc," that kind of thing. I am trying not to show my irritation. I like Allegra and her private school manners. All week I have been carrying around a book of Rumi's poems she gave me and wearing an orange and black autumn harvest Hermès scarf that she helped Carl pick out for a Christmas present. I wish I had not known that the present was Allegra's idea. They met a few weeks before Carl got his diagnosis, and Allegra, a forty-something who has never married, is in the delicate position of having to navigate territory that is completely foreign to her. Anyway, she's exhausted from three productions she has worked on and feeling the strain of trying to keep Carl propped up.

"You really should get a neighbor to watch your house," she tells me in the car on our way to Central Market. I immediately react and want to say to her, *I have raised kids and lived all over the world in many houses and apartments,* but 2002 has brought a fresh wave of resolutions including to try to channel compassion to one and all, as if my yoga teacher's closing meditation, *you have everything you need,* is reality and not wishful thinking.

We are splitting a carrot cake when Carl flops down beside us. "We are going to China," he says. "I am going to be treated by the dragons. That's what they call the master doctors there."

Carl begins to shout in the middle of the café: "You are not to call one single person! No *New York Times* bureau chief! No China experts from New York! I don't care who you are or what you know. This is dangerous! I could get arrested for being treated in China." He looks nervously around the café, then stabs his fork into the cake. "You don't need to eat this," he says.

It is 2002 and everyone knows that China is opening up wide.

"People go in and out all the time," I say. "You think anyone cares where you go?"

"No one is to know," he says. "And another thing. I don't want you harassing the doctors if you go. I'll be the one to ask the questions."

But asking questions is what I do best. It becomes the career of anyone in this situation. That is, in fact, almost all one can do. We are exploring the world of clinical trials, sending flurries of e-mails to anyone who could help us, trying to get access to the high and the mighty at university hospitals and the National Institutes of Health.

There is an undercurrent at the table. Carl and Allegra have just returned from a Christmas in Istanbul, boat rides on the Bosporus. We had a shouting match as he left. "You must have your spleen removed," I said angrily. "You don't have time to take two weeks in Turkey." Allegra has lobbied him to travel, urging him to relax, have a baby, and see the world. I was doing what members of families do, believing that I knew what was best for my brother, if only he would listen to me. "Every single doctor you have been speaking to has told you the same damn thing," I said. "Find a treatment and stick to it."

But from Johns Hopkins to Duke to Houston, Carl has asked specialists what can be done to beat this cancer back.

Not much, is always the answer.

Allegra surely was right.

I am on the telephone with my friend Joe, who is helping us. The other line rings and it is Carl. I get off with Joe and say to Carl, "That was Joe. He sends his love to you." There is a sudden tense quiet on the telephone.

In that silence is the warning shot across the bow: Here you go again.

I get ready for the rage that is on its way.

"I want to start this year on a new note. Your friend Joe doesn't know me. Why would he send me his love?"

"That's what he said," I say. "I taped the call."

"You did not."

"You're right. I didn't."

"WHY DO YOU ALWAYS EXAGGERATE EVERY-THING?"

"I did not exaggerate. He sent you his love."

"I want it plain. I don't want all this New York bullshit. He might have said send him my best or tell him hello, but he sure did not send me his love. Why are you always so filled with hyperbole? You are such a phony." Then he slams the phone down.

Is Carl right?

Is Carl wrong?

Why is this such a terrible thing?

I could not say what I really feel. That I am desperate and afraid.

Beijing is gray and overcast from the air, but as we land, twenty-six hours on the plane from New York through Korea, a clear blue sky opens up. Crowds of bicyclists come at us in unending waves. Carl and Allegra are already set up in the St. Regis Hotel, a five-star that is overrun with Secret Service preparing for a visit by George W. Bush the following week.

Carl meets us in the lobby, filled with energy. "Get in the car," he says. "There is something you have to see." I am cranky from the long flight. With me are stacks of tapes on the Enron scandal, a story I am working on. On a six-hour layover in Seoul, Ernie works his way through the lounge dim sum and the duty-free, and I am desperately trying to transcribe interviews with the women of Enron who have been witnesses to Ken Lay's chicanery.

"I am not up for the Great Wall today. Forget it."

"Who the hell wants the Great Wall? We can do that tomorrow. Get in the car."

We are now in a massive Beijing traffic jam, looking at construction and the pollution coming from the direction of the palace. Beijing seems to be doubling in front of us, there are so many crews and trucks out working. Everyone is smoking, smoking on bikes.

Ahead of us looms Carrefour, a large French supermarket chain. "They're selling our apples!" Carl says.

We make our way through the crowds of dour Asians filling their baskets with elaborate oversized cellophane packs.

Soon Carl is standing in front of a hill of perfect red apples stamped with the red Washington Apple sticker, his code on the tag. "This won't last long," Ernie says. "The Chinese are leaving millions of apples in their fields. They will kill the American fruit market."

A shadow crosses Carl's face. "Yeah, well, they won't grow an apple that tastes like these," he said.

"Costco won't care," Ernie says.

So, we are a million miles away, arguing about globalization in a Carrefour in Beijing. I look over and see that Carl's shirt is wet. "What is that?" I ask.

"Scorpion patches."

Then he scrunches his face up, like, You idiot. "That's what the dragons do here," he says. "They come to the hotel room and put on these hot patches of poisons. They sweat out the toxin." He pulls up his shirt in the middle of the check-out line. The crowd looks at us, trying to understand what these crazy foreigners are doing in the middle of their supermarket. Carl's skin has bright red patches, as if he has a bad sunburn. "That's what the patches do. They make you really burn. But they do work. They will make me cancer free." He looks at me as if he expects another argument, a version of what the hell are you doing in this backward country when you should be having radiation in New York?

"You need to have your spleen out," I say. "This is crazy."

Allegra stares me down. "Say something," I tell her. "I am trying to get his head on straight."

"He has a lot of confidence in the herbs," she says, steadily. "Dr. Wong believes they are working."

We were suddenly moving north, toward the Great Wall. Jet lag was setting in and it was hard to focus on the looming landmark that cut a ribbon through the China mountains. Tourist buses crowded the parking lot Carl and Allegra and Ernie loped ahead, up the steps, and suddenly we were on top of the wall, posing in front of a sign that read YOU HAVE CLIMBED THE GREAT WALL OF CHINA.

Now Allegra and Ernie were racing fast up the wall, which has a quality of a wide sidewalk over a fortress. You could see it snake for miles, about four thousand by some estimates, up and down through northern China. We were silent, taken in by actually being on a wonder of the world.

I walked with Carl, holding on to his arm, enjoying the miracle of us being together, the shiver of January weather in the mountains. "You are amazing," I said. "Do you know that?"

Carl was quiet.

"I need to go back to the car," he said. He was breathing hard.

I looked over to see liquid running down his shirt.

"The goddamn patches. They're burning me. Something is leaking. They didn't tape them correctly."

Suddenly, he collapsed against the wall.

"Don't let Allegra see me," he said. "I don't want her to know."

We made our way through the horde of tour buses, then sat in the SUV. Soon, Allegra and Ernie came bounding down the long steps. "Is anything the matter?"

"Just a leak, no big deal."

I was quiet but telegraphed *trouble* to Ernie.

"You go on," Carl said. "Marie and I will wait here."

There was a moment of hesitation. Then Allegra said, "Okay. How many times will I get to China and the Great Wall?"

We watched them disappear up the canyon heading toward Mongolia.

Carl shut his eyes and looked teary. He dozed a few moments.

"Maybe this trip wasn't such a great idea."

"You don't know that," I said.

He reached over to get a carefully detailed list written on a legal pad out of his briefcase.

"Let's come up with a schedule for the next twelve months," he said. "There are clinical trials all over America. Gene vaccines. New medications all the time. We need to look at everything. I need your help. I really really do."

I did not know what to say.

"You're my sister," he said, his voice catching.

3 8

Another letter from the files.

July 10, 1990

Dear Marie and Carl,

When it comes time to bury me, please, no funerals!

I want to be cremated. The urn containing the ashes should be buried in the designated space to the immediate south of your mother.

A long-nosed shovel or post-hole digger can create the space in a few minutes. Anyone can do it, and no religious service or permit is required.

I suggest that you have a reception for friends (yours and mine), serving refreshments and snacks. A Tchaikovsky and Rimsky-Korsakov program would be preferred.

Some may want to say a few words. I want no clergy or rabbi to speak. No rabbis! I want no prayers or religious ceremony. I want a strictly secular family reception.

I love you,
Dad

And in case we missed the urgency he signed it again: *Milton C. Brenner.*

39

Positive thoughts.

I will keep saying everything is okay. I will be cheerful and reasonable and not stare at the apple wallpaper, trying to figure out what excuse I can use to get out of here and get back to New York. I will not be negative. Just this once, in my life, today, for example, I will be content in my skin. I will force myself to use words I hear on daytime TV—the gift, the lesson, the miracle. I will repeat to myself that every day I get up, I will say a little prayer of gratitude. I will count my blessings. I will list in a gratitude journal everything to be thankful for. I will run three miles. I will admit I am in error and misinformed at all times.

What is going wrong here? I ask my friend Deeda, who has been tutoring us on what is available in clinical trials. There's a pause on the telephone, then Deeda, schooled in a time when women spoke in whispers, suggests, "Perhaps you are sounding too competent. Try to show him you too are afraid. It might cause him to open up."

I speak to Deeda almost every day. "I have someone who might be able to help your crazy brother," my friend Jane in

Washington told me soon after she learned about Carl. "Her name is Deeda Blair." I knew of her only as a figure in the columns, a woman of style with famous friends and a vast closet of Chanel and Ralph Rucci couture. "How can she possibly help?" I asked. "She knows more about medicine than almost anyone in the country," Jane said. As a young woman, Deeda assisted Mary Lasker at a time when Lyndon Johnson had tapped Lasker to work on his war on cancer, and she soon emerged on the cutting edge of medical research. Now, thirty years later, she had raised millions of dollars for the Harvard AIDS Institute and was an advocate for the National Institutes of Health. She is something else as well, an elegant presence with a heart as big as the moon, reaching out to dozens of people privately to help them through the nightmare and labyrinth of the cancer world.

And all of it done with such lightness, a perfect touch.

Soon after Deeda speaks to Carl for the first time, I call him. "What are you doing?" I ask, hearing his Cuisinart.

"I'm making a recipe. Something your friend Deeda sent me in a fax. It's great. I make it almost every day."

"A recipe?"

"An apple thing," he said. "Deeda really understands my fruit."

Healthy Chopped Apples

Take Honeycrisp apples—wash and cut in quarters, remove cores but do not peel—throw in Cuisinart.

Add:

Several squeezes of lemon

TINY bits of sugar and CHOP

It should not become a puree. Put in bowls and sprinkle with cinnamon.

40

A few random items I find in a folder marked "Carl, 1970s."

A photo, soon after my first article is published: "To the world's best authoress . . ." I have dozens of these pictures: Carl with his foot on a bloody carcass, smiling in victory, the sun gleaming off his glasses. Carl in camouflage clothes, feathers and fur and animal blood staining his khakis.

February 20, 1973
Dear Marie,
March 2nd is Texas Independence Day. If you want to have a little party for some Texans and a few non-Texans that night, I'll be glad to help you out. I will be stopping in the city on my way to Africa. Alternately, if you want to cook a few doves or some venison for a small group, then I can bring some on the airplane.
Congratulations on your raise.

Love,
Carl

P.S. I wrote Pat Ewing for a date that night and I'm reason-ably sure that she won't have any other plans.

Leopard Attack After Attack on Man

Chronicle, *Bulawayo, Rhodesia*

An African assistant, Mr. Gumbo, was mauled by a wounded leopard during a hunting attack in the Matetsi area on Saturday. Although bitten in the shoulder and hand, he is not in a serious condition. . . .

An American, Mr. Carl Brenner, 26, and his father, Mr. Milton Brenner, who are on safari organized by Mr. Robinson and professional hunter Mr. Rob Mann, were out hunting at the time.

The Americans had come to Rhodesia to hunt leopard.

Mr. Robinson said yesterday that Mr. Milton Brenner came on the leopard after it made a kill at about 5:00 p.m. on Friday. He shot and wounded it.

"The animal disappeared into long grass and reeds. On Saturday morning the Brenners, Mr. Mann and I went to track down the wounded leopard. We had some anxious moments in the high grass as the leopard sprang about a lot," Mr. Robinson said.

". . . We continued tracking it, and it came out of the grass where Mr. Carl Brenner shot and killed it."

Mr. Carl Brenner, from San Antonio, Texas, bagged a 10 year old male leopard on Wednesday which measured 2:25 m., a Rhodesian record. The big leopard had been tracked by Mr. Brenner and Mr. Mann for a week.

Mr. Brenner had successfully hunted a number of species of antelope in Mozambique and lion and buffalo in Tanzania in 1971. He made his record kill at 6:00 p.m. on Wednesday when the large animal was 90 m. away. It was running toward a tree after it made a kill. Mr. Brenner has also bagged a waterbuck with horns slightly less than a metre and a sable with horns measuring 1.5 m.

The faded photocopy fell out of an album that had come from a Texas warehouse. The news is at the top of the fold in Rhodesia that day, sharing pride of place with the headline, "Nixon Impeachment Demand, New USA Crisis." Carl and Milton and Richard Nixon, top of the fold, October 22, 1973. The image was irresistible: Carl, at twenty-six, bagging a record leopard, almost killed in the process. Snarling animals and Jewish Texans with their elephant guns and ranch khakis. A father and son holiday, one of many. Carl, just out of law school, celebrating a high score on the bar. That made the papers too. Our father saw to that. The clipping fluttered out, neatly filed as it had been in the same box. At this moment in his life, he is in lockstep with his father, acting out what it means to be the firstborn son.

Carl saw his first apple orchards in Africa.

1975. One day, he took off and did not come back for weeks. *I'm going to Africa*, he said. *I need to get away.* He scrimped and saved and bought a coach ticket from a bargain agency and prepared himself for the twenty-four-hour flight. He would stop in the small island of Sal to refuel, then get back on the plane and land in Jo-Berg, as he now called it, as if to impress us all with his new intimate knowledge of foreign cities. It was a time in his life when he was trying to kick off the traces, touring the wine country and ordering elaborate Bordeaux at dinner, then sloshing it through his teeth.

"Stop doing that," I said. "It's revolting."

"What do you know?" he said. "That's how they do it at the Taste du Vin. I've been to Bordeaux and I know."

I understood Carl's restless nature, his need to fly here and there. We shared that trait, finding ourselves in new experiences, questions shelved.

A few years later, he would be hired by a group of South Texas peanut farmers in a class-action suit. Every day he drove to a ranch town, drowning in litigation involving farmers allegedly getting shorted by the makers of Skippy peanut butter. (The case was later settled.) He was thirty-two years old, living the life that was expected of him, of suits from Brooks Brothers, and dinners on the San Antonio River at the Club Giraud. He worried about the limits of all of this, about becoming a stopped person. He wondered on the telephone if married life ultimately becomes "two people who only talk about the quality of the steak."

By this time, I had already been in New York, trying to find my own way. "I am going to be a writer," I announced weakly to a friend of my parents who sat next to me on a Braniff Airways flight from San Antonio to LaGuardia. Did he notice the panic in my voice? The stewardess wore a Pucci and I had on my turquoise miniskirt. Within weeks, I had a job in the arbitrage department of Goldman Sachs. The chairman of Goldman Sachs arrived at my apartment one day with bags of LPs. Not knowing better, I invited him up, then pushed him when he tried to French-kiss me. *Don't you have a grandson?* One day I walked into the bathroom at work and saw a beautiful blonde crying at the sink. "The men here are such misogynists! I am quitting and going back to grad school!"

Me too! I said, because I've always given an immediate yes to anything that sounds like a good idea.

The truth is, I did not have a choice. "You can't add anything," my boss, a handsome thirty-year-old from Miami named Robert Rubin, said angrily. He went on to be Clinton's secretary of the treasury.

It was a confusing time. On our first day in arbitrage, some of the interns were given their marching orders by a few of the bosses: *Call up anyone you went to school with and find out what deals they are working on.* It was explained to us that our value would be enhanced by how much we could uncover so our bosses could trade the stocks, making money on the spreads. Later, this practice, commonplace on Wall Street, sent dozens to jail for trading on inside information.

I was twenty-two years old, lurching from job to job, then got engaged to a young man from Fort Worth who worked for McKinsey and Company. He had a kind face and curly hair, and was confident of his future. He proposed and I said yes. It seemed like a good idea at the time, a ride into a more certain future. He took me to see his mother. She looked like the women at our temple and presented me with boxes of greeting cards that she had already stamped to send out to dozens of family cousins. "I always remember everyone's birthdays. You can if you are organized," she said, looking at me sharply. "I keep all the relatives on file."

"I want to be a writer," I said.

"You'll be a great hostess," my fiancé answered. Then I gained fifteen pounds.

"Something is not right here," my mother said. "What are you doing?" The wedding invitations were in the mail, hundreds of them, an elaborate gala set for the Argyle Club in San Antonio. In New York, the women were marching up and down Fifth Avenue. "I can't do this," I said.

I found a way into grad school.

"Marie will be home in a year," Carl said. "She will never make it in New York."

Near the Museum of Modern Art, a girl with long braids was selling Italian ices from a cart. "How much do you make on a good day?" I asked her. "About fifty dollars," she said. That was more than I needed. "Where do you get the cart?" I asked. I was on Eleventh Avenue negotiating with Johnny, the Greek King of Ice. He wore a fishnet T-shirt and had a gold cross dangling from his neck. Central Park was staked cut by the concessionaires—the Greek ice cream mafia. Every morning that summer I trudged back to Eleventh Avenue to pick up my cart and then wheeled it up to the park. I was confined to a spot near the Delacorte Theater. For weeks, I took notes on the buying patterns of the clientele. Who knew that WASPs on Fifth Avenue always took lemon and the West Siders preferred chocolate? It was hot and difficult work, with vast stretches of empty time. I was furious and exhausted, and on one memorable day, I tried to push the cart into the pond. I came home to my small apartment and began typing "Confessions of a Pushcart Peddler." I sent it over the transom, more or less, to a tall red-haired editor at *New York* magazine I had met at a party. He was from Texas and felt sorry for me. "My name is Aaron Latham, and if you ever write anything, send it to me." A few days later, he called me. "Well, we can't pay you much—only three hundred dollars—but everyone likes it here."

It was the beginning of my career. In San Antonio, my father carried the issue with him everywhere. I was now a reporter.

Not long after, Carl was in New York. "Daddy's gone nuts," he said. "You cannot believe these crazy memos he's sending me." Every day they fought about property, they fought about store policies, they fought about larger issues that were unexpressed. "He tries to control everything," he said.

"You don't have to do this," I said. "Move away. You have a law degree."

"I can't," Carl said. "You have no idea what is expected of me."

41

Carl had never shown an interest in a shrub or a plant. There was no sense that he cared anything about horticulture or gardening or the cultivation of fruit. But then, in Africa, flying low over the Cape Dutch country, he saw it: a carpet of trees. Apple blossom time in the apple country. A fruit set on the trees, pink froth of bloom everywhere. He stayed through the summer and into the fall.

"This is God's country," he said, his voice finally relaxing in our weekly calls. He had found his way to the apple country near the Cape wine country and was immersed in setting up his trees. He would return to America with sketches of all of his pickers' feet and fill suitcases with jogging shoes to fit them. "There is so much to be done here," he said, bursting suddenly with life, his own man at last.

It is soon after Casey is born. On the telephone, he is raving about it, bubbling over with what he has seen. I thought he was a lunatic. From the moment Casey appears, she is the center of my life, next to me on a pillow as an infant, strapped to me as I type.

It is an era in New York of pouf skirts and the rise of Donald Trump. Nancy Reagan had just taken her china to Washington. The phone rang constantly. I was thirty-two, living in a duplex in Chelsea, in love with my husband, and had an infant in my arms. Carl was very far away.

42

"None of this is going to work, you know," Carl says. "These people here are just whistling in the dark." We are driving past the turnoff to Slidewaters, the local water park, the lake pooling in front of us. Tiny green vines cover a hillside, and Carl is sounding off on the plans of the apple orchardists to turn the apple country into Napa. "They're planting grapes!" Carl says. "Who has ever heard of anything more ridiculous? They think this place is going to attract people like the Napa Valley. These apple farmers at the Apple Cup sit around and tell you that it is the same latitude as Bordeaux."

I read to Carl the headlines from that month's *Good Fruit*. It is just after dawn and we are walking the orchard lanes in Cashmere as the pickers shake off the morning frost from their silver ladders and arrange them in the trees. It is the day when they will finish the Galas. The red wood bins are in the middle of each row, filling with fruit, gleaming in the sun. Carl walks ahead of me, his pace long and strong. The quiet closes around me. All I hear is birdsong. Suddenly, the colors of the leaves are all I see. There are greens of every kind, citron green and mossy green and the green of the inside of a gentlemen's club. It is a moment when the apple country is no longer foreign or tedious but something else, something of its own. For the smallest moment, I am able to put my big fat ego into a closet. Another feeling is coming over me, a higher place. Everything came into a kind of blankness, as if I were a screen where I could just take in everybody's everything and it was all okay. I can feel Carl's terror and loneliness and need.

And then my cell phone rings. It's my friend Lowell, calling from the East.

"I'm sorry your brother died," he said.

"Died?"

"I heard he died."

"What are you talking about? He is right here with me at his apple harvest. He's in *perfect* shape. At the moment, I cannot keep up with him. That's what good shape he's in. He has more energy than I do. We're out here picking fruit."

"Jesus," Lowell says. "I'm sorry. I shouldn't have called."

"I gotta go," I say quietly. "He is fine. I wish I had his energy. He is a complete inspiration."

I hang up, convinced that what I have just said is true.

43

Carl bangs on the door of my room. It is four-thirty a.m. He has tears in his eyes. "They have screwed up my fruit. Black spots have turned up on the Asians."

He holds one in his hand and puts a box on the floor. There's a kitchenette with one of those motel coffee machines. *Look,* he says, *everything is ruined.* The brown fuzzy fruits are lined up. He takes a knife and cuts them, one after another. Each one is marbled inside with ink blots, spot after spot. Tears stream down his face.

"Some son of a bitch at the cold storage! He did this to me! He did this to my fruit! Everything is going to come back. Central Market, Wegmans! They are all going to return everything! This is all because of my medical! They kept the fruit at twenty-nine degrees!"

I move to put my arms around him but he bridles and backs away. "It's because of my medical. I wasn't here to watch the crop," he says.

"Come on," he says. "Get in the truck. Throw on your clothes. We have to get to the storage plant."

The coffee from the 7-Eleven burns my hand. I close my eyes and count backward, trying a meditation technique. See yourself as a four-year-old, someone taught me, and treat yourself with the same gentleness with which you would treat that child.

I am counting backward, looking for that four-year-old. None of it is working.

I have my notebook with me.

"Tell me what bitter pit is exactly?" I ask, prepared to take notes.

"Can you stop doing that?" he says, suddenly furious. "I have no time to teach."

Bitter pit: a disease caused by the lack of calcium or excessive magnesium or potassium in the fruit.

Apple scab: a fungus that leaves brown lesions on the skin.

And in case you ever have an orchard:

Codling moth: a bug that accounts for the most damage done to apples.

Later that morning, I make up an excuse and tell Carl that I will see him later at the packinghouse. I want to go to Starbucks and read the *Times*. The weather has turned colder in the Cascades. I want to be back in my own life, not thinking about my brother or forcing myself to learn apple terms. I have monkey mind, the thoughts skittering this way and that.

I've waited long enough, dawdled at Smitty's with the morning *Wenatchee World*, driven past the Cascadian packinghouse with its faded murals of pears and apples barely visible on the outside walls. You could not spend two days here without noticing the ghostlike quality of farm country frozen in time.

How unusual. Carl is at the gym. He's on the elliptical machine across the floor, reading. He's pounding it hard, sweat flying. I strain to see what is on the machine. It's the Luther Burbank biography. I wonder if he has seen the photo of Burbank sitting on a step with Henry Ford, one of the hundreds of celebrities who made their way to Santa Rosa, California, to walk his orchards and see the eight hundred strains of plants he had developed. At the height of his fame, he came up with 113 varieties of plums and prunes, two dozen blackberries and raspberries, and one type of almond.

I watch Carl silently from across the floor. He's managing to ignore the feed from Afghanistan. Anyone looking at Carl would think he is in perfect health.

Suddenly, I am overwhelmed by how much I love him. It seems inconceivable that we are connected, and yet not. Inconceivable how he is able to pursue the dailiness of his life—the ordinary small stuff, like taking his book to the gym—no matter what it takes, just to get in and claim it without anyone slowing down the process.

I run into the locker room short of breath, unable to keep my balance. No one seems to mind. The women of Wenatchee gather around me, naked and pillowy and comforting. I can't tell them the truth, which is that I have a brother who is going to die. He'd kill me. He likes his image of the Texas loner who flies in and out. I try to focus on my breath, a yoga trick. In and out; in, out. Not easy. My brother, with his red-faced opinions, is now a man thrashing in a lake, trying to squeeze a life into every single day.

44

Late afternoon, Wenatchee.

I need to tell you something.

We are in the truck passing the Washington Pick 'n Pay. I sit in the back, Carl and Ernie in the front. We've just passed the Economy Motel and the sign that says GOD BLESS AMERICA. Ernie is trying to ask Carl a lot of Carl questions but isn't paying attention to the answers. Ernie's on his BlackBerry as usual, trying to schedule airplane flights. It's what he does when he doesn't want to be somewhere, starts making plans about how to be somewhere else. Who can blame him?

Soon after I was divorced, we met on a blind date in New York set up by one of his partners. Who knew we both came from the same hometown? I was thirty-five years old and racing from assignment to assignment for *New York* magazine. "He can't be from San Antonio," I said. "My mother would have sent me a note. He has to be from one of the other towns in the area, Austin or Seguin." What was I talking about? Wrong again.

On our first date, we squabbled about people we knew in common. On our second date, Ernie, a gifted cook, sculpted tomato roses. Love is like that: you see something in someone that reminds you of everything familiar, but viewed suddenly in an entirely different way. We were married within a year of our first date. He's a specialist in foreign markets and travels the world, absorbing all that is new. I am in awe of how he shows up to take care of everything. There are many days when we both wonder, What are we doing here? Then we go to dinner. I guess love is like that too.

The morning has been spent with my brother looking deeply into Ernie's face and telling him that he should give over significant portions of his life to maintaining Carl's apple business. I know you don't like details, Carl tells him. Well, with apples, details are all there is. It's so much like Carl, needy and infuriating, and I watch Ernie vaporize, not wanting to disagree. I'll do whatever I can to help, he says, with no heart in his voice. He's another firstborn, seeming to walk around with a sack of stones and the absolute belief that his path is the right one.

Then, Carl says, *I have been reading a lot about Christianity.*

That's nice.

I have been studying the New Testament.

Carl clears his throat. Out the window I notice a cherry grove.

You know there is no difference between the Jewish belief in God and the Christian except that Jews pray to God directly and Christians use the vehicle of Jesus. I want you to know that the other day I confessed my sins to Jesus.

The atmosphere in the car has turned sour. What was it about Jesus that brought this on? Carl is on a search for meaning in his life, in my life, in life itself, but the search has not taken the Carlness out if it, the belligerence, the coming at you with the hard little eyes of moral superiority like he was onto something that you aren't. Was his search bringing him peace or contentment or something that was, well, spiritual? Spiritual usually means that your voice drops and you project a higher wisdom, saying God-like mantras like, May your suffering lift. I know what he is looking for, I think. Perhaps something to tell him that his life has a meaning, that it has been about something, that there will be a reason for all of the wrong steps and wasted time and stupid stuff and moments where he could have changed that or embraced that or taken more care with that. That he could see his life as whole and beautiful and having had a perfect balance of kindness and that the rush of nerves and anger, the wildness of the thought train that is out of control could be brought under control with the help of Jesus and learning the parable of the Woman at the Well. It was an elevation, a noble task to make the next weeks and months and hard choices easier, small beer in comparison to what Jesus had gone through on the cross. And that if he prayed his way through it, struggled for faith or something inside that all of his rational, secular, Reformed Jewish brain fought against, if he could reach for something new and rare, that would be a new place. That the kindness and the grace of the church could bring out his own kindness and grace.

I don't react at all. His wanderings with God and the born-agains and thinking about Jesus startle me, but everything about Carl suddenly startles me, from the moment I saw him staring down the thousands of shiny red apples bobbing at him in the packinghouse. It was all new, the humanness of my brother. I study him as he looks under toadstools for enlightenment or something to explain the universe. We were both struggling with some way to get the barricade to lift, to have an actual conversation, a talk without the cotton wool around it, clogging the moments.

I may not be here in a year, he says.

Silence from the front seat.

I have the dinner in the back. The fish we are bringing is a kind of trout that, I have been told, morphs from one variety to another, depending on whether it's in salt water or fresh water. I am reading a lot of symbolism into that.

We are having dinner with the head of the local land trust and his wife.

Whatever you do, don't bring up the subject of adoption, Carl says, suddenly changing the subject. Linda is adopted and the topic is taboo. Again, the scowl, the need to put the censor on me.

Don't speak.

Why are you wearing so much jewelry?

Keep it simple.

By the time we drive through the last line of cherry trees, I am a wreck, teary and angry. What I remember most about the drive is the look, the torch job, and the feeling that in introducing this huge topic, this risky business that is so profound in his life, he has the need to be Carl, not peaceful and into the struggle toward spirituality, but spiritual like an angry prophet, a Jeremiah of doom, a Moses yelling at the Israelites and waving the tablets above his head. And if the religion was really there to fill him with golden light, to answer these questions of self and why we are all here and what the higher purpose of life is, then maybe his higher purpose was that he was angry and powerful and striving and working in overdrive, and was there anything wrong with that? Wasn't that Carlness as holy and human as someone else's lack of attachment?

Linda greets me with a cheerful hug. "I've found my birth mother! She's an artist. . . . What an amazing experience it has been!"

4 5

. . . .

I am not good with quaint. Or towns where people brake for you when you jaywalk, watch you so closely that they know you are about to cross the street. You stand on a curb and suddenly the traffic slows down and they motion to you, cross here, cross now. All that country courtesy is unnerving, feels suspicious.

And then the noise. City people have a belief that the country people live some sort of ideal quiet life. This is fixed in the brain of anyone in a city who has not spent more than three days actually living in the middle of a country town. There, it is a swarm of noise, of buzz saws out a window where they are doing constant repairs, shutter cutting, motorcycle racing, road repaving, beeps of trucks and engines sawing up and down streets with names like Court Lane all night long.

So I drive in the apple country, trying to get away from the din of the ten-wheelers, the road repairers, and Sam, the shutter sawer who greets me with a cheery, Morning! as he moves his buzz saw outside the window and sets up his wooden sawhorses at six a.m.

A voice comes on the radio: "God does not call his children to live in the Mojave. And your desert is not Palm Springs. It might be ill health that stays with you for a long period of time. It is that which brings personal pain or hardship—that is the desert. It may be a broken romance or divorce. The desert wears many clothes. That is your calling. In Deuteronomy 32 we have a direct reference to Israel. 'He found him in a desert land.'"

The minister has the twang of a fundamentalist, a Bible-thumping, abortion-hating Jew-baiter. I hate these people and the trouble they cause, the parishioners they knock up, the pedophilia they hide, the wars they create. How can anyone believe that the God Squad has the answer to anything? Why am I listening?

"Technically, the 'him' is a reference to the Jews. Please substitute your name for him—who God found in the desert."

Is this what my brother listens to alone in his room?

I glide along, watching the signs roll by. There is the turnoff for the Ohme Gardens, an alpine den of cedars and rocks in the shadow of the McDougall packinghouse. I push the radio buttons, preset, then peer at the dashboard for the scan. Why are these cars so impossible? Why is there no simple button to twirl? Does everything in America need a remote control that only a geek can figure out?

"One authoritative group, using worst-case assumptions, estimated that a plane spreading anthrax over a big city might kill one hundred thousand people. Another suggested that it might even be three million. . . . Panicky citizens have been trying to obtain and hoard Cipro or other drugs to use in case the unthinkable happens."

No wonder Carl chooses to spend large chunks of time here. You can drive into Chelan and not think about the unthinkable. You can just be.

4 6

The following is not unrelated to this story:

I hear the words when I'm twenty-eight years old: You have malignant cancer. You have a cancer that is so dangerous it could kill you. You could die of this.

And this: You must come home to Texas immediately and have surgery.

I am on my way to India. It is my first trip. I am reading and underlining V. S. Naipaul. "A Resting-Place for the Imagination," Naipaul names the opening chapter of *An Area of Darkness*. The idea of India pulls me across and out of my life. I write down Naipaul's descriptions: "As soon as our quarantine flag came down and the last of the barefooted, blue-uniformed policemen of the Bombay Port Health Authority had left the ship, Coelho the Goan came aboard and, luring me with a long beckoning finger into the saloon, whispered, 'You have any cheej?'" Naipaul continues, "He required cheese. It was a delicacy in India. Imports were restricted, and the Indians had not yet learned how to make cheese, just as they had not yet learned how to bleach newsprint."

I insist that I will be fine, take twenty shots, and imagine myself in a hut in the Thar desert with women who wear veils of red and pink and gold rings in their noses. I want to create something for myself that is wholly unpredicted. By then, I have written for magazines and turned out a trashy novel that makes just enough money to allow me to live in London. The pound is weak against the dollar and it is possible to do that, to spend half of what it would cost to live in New York. I borrow flats, affect Pan-European mannerisms like putting the day in front of the month: 16 July 1978. "I know you will be all right when you stop doing that," my friend Nora writes. I struggle every day with trying to get published. And then suddenly an exotic assignment from an English newspaper. I am just coming to the point in a young career when editors would call me and assign me to go places and talk to people and I would get paid to write about it. I could say into the telephone now to my mother, "I can't talk! I'm working on a piece!" I could rush into subways and tell editors, I need a plane, a train, more time.

And then: You have cancer.

And this: If you do not cancel that goddamn trip to that filthy country, you will be dead by the age of thirty.

Soon I am in a hospital reading photocopies of articles about this fatal thing, melanoma. I am ushered into the oncology department. There is the hospital smell, the color of the doctors' gowns, the feeling that my life is not going to come back. I am told the score. This cancer is a killer. If I do not have it excised, I will not live to see thirty-five. I hear these words: *There is no cure.* My mother sits at the bed and cries. But melanoma is an odd one. You do not feel any different than you did the day before. It sits on top of your skin like any other mole, until it's not. It looks like a nothing, a tiny blue streak of ink on your back. I am on the telephone with my best friend, Annie. I am weeping. "I am going to die," I say. "And I'm not even married yet." I do not know any-one my age who has died of cancer.

Carl is in the room, shouting. "Don't tell anyone what you have," he says. "They will have you dead and buried by the time you get back to New York. Hang up right now!"

Get out of this room! I scream. You have no right to tell me what I can tell my friends!

I wind up with a hole in my back. "How could you have done this to her?" my mother says to the surgeon, who happens to be a cousin. "Marie will never get to wear another strapless dress!"

Soon I move back to America, saved by a tabloid editor named Don Forst who takes over the *Boston Herald American*. India with its lack of sanitation is no longer a reasonable destina-tion. They have made me believe that. "You're sounding like an ex-pat with that stupid accent," he says. "Come to Boston and write about the Red Sox. They're letting women in the clubhouse for the first time." "I've never been to a major league game," I say. A pause. "Well, you'll have a fresh eye on the sport." I would go to the ballpark and try to understand what I was doing in a city where I knew almost no one, writing about a subject that I knew nothing about. I am still reading V. S. Naipaul. "Adventure is possible. But a knowledge of degree is in the bones and no Indian is far from his origins. It is like a physical yearning: the tycoon in his cubby-hole, the entrepreneur clerk sleeping on the pavement, the Brahmin leather-goods manufacturers anxious to protect their children against caste contamination." I live in a sublet of a house on Marlboro Street where the owner, a landscape architect, had designed a famous garden of laminate bagels laid out on lavender gravel.

I spend weeks thinking about suicide and eat and throw up a quart of ice cream most nights. I am desperate to try to get back in control of my life, to get a life at all. Every day I ride my bike to Fenway Park and chain it on Yawkey Way. The sound of batting practice swallows me up from the moment I come down the ramps and see the green field through the tunnel. I stand with the other sportswriters watching the Red Sox, feeling lucky and completely saved. Baseball babble occupies me for weeks. I've joined a team of white superstars—baseball legends like Carl Yastrzemski and Carlton Fisk. It is a summer when everything is changing in the major leagues. I don't know enough about the sport to write about the players, so my attention turns to the stands. "Why are there no blacks here?" I ask one of the writers. "At Fenway? Are you kidding? This is Boston." "Why are there no blacks at Fenway Park?" I interview a few I find. The column runs and soon after I'm in the clubhouse. A tape ball comes hurling at my head, pitched by the right fielder Dwight Evans. It misses, which I tell myself was deliberate. *Get the hell out of here,* he says.

Soon after that I meet my first husband.

Press box, Yankee Stadium:

"I know you," I say. I had met him once at a party and knew he was a beautiful writer and unusual radio personality, known as "the voice" in certain circles in New York.

"You do?"

He has a radio voice, soft and articulate, uses the names Saul Bellow and Joan Didion in conversation. I know he has recently published a novel and mention this to him, hoping he will not ask me if I have read it. He does. "Yes," I say. "What did you think of it?" The first word that occurs to me is "elliptical." What am I talking about? I do not even know exactly what it means. All at midnight in Yankee Stadium, the flow.

I have a pencil in my mouth.

The game goes to fourteen innings.

Two a.m. And I still have to file.

I'll call you, he says.

But first he says, "What? You travel with the Boston Red Sox? You are that idiot that is writing the Red Sox Diary in the *Boston Herald American*? They have given you a page-one column because you are *a girl*?"

"Yes."

Life is a bitter mystery, he says.

Do you read my columns? I ask.

I am afraid I do, he says.

There is no malice in his remark.

Soon we are at Fenway Park. "Isn't this beautiful? Even the British think so." He looks out at the diamond, the white lines bright. He resembles the writer Philip Roth, and my first thought is: Jonathan Schwartz is a Red Sox lunatic. His friends call him Jonno. I saw him for the first time a few years before when I was new to New York, at a tennis party on a Westchester estate. Who is that man? I asked a friend who brought me. He was deeply tan, gesturing wildly on a chaise. The image stayed with me. And his name. "That's Jonathan Schwartz. He's on the radio. He knows so much about music and everything." It took seven years for our paths to cross again. Is anything in life an accident? He had a vibrant inner life, the smile of a delighted child, a dark intensity that could blow you over or lift you, depending on the wind. His passions drew me in.

"If they lose this game, that's IT!" he says, leaning against the rail.

You know everything about a man within the first two weeks. That was my mother's rule.

Within three months we are married. At the wedding, there are life-sized piñatas of Red Sox uniforms. My mother has them made by the piñata man in the barrio of San Antonio.

Carl does not come to the wedding.

You changed the date, he said.

The cancer has yet to reappear.

Say yes to everything, Cole Porter said.

Jonathan taught me that.

47

September 2, 1982. The Red Sox are at Yankee Stadium. I am overdue in labor.

"I will not wait another day," Jonathan says. Our doctor says, "So take a long walk. That usually works." "It's too humid for me," Jonathan says. My mother is with me. "We'll go," I say. "It's just weather."

We walk to Bloomingdale's from East Seventy-second Street, the doctor's office. It's murderously humid. By the time we hit Fifty-ninth Street, I'm in labor.

I have written a story on Henry Kissinger. I write snide comments about his arrival in New York. I am especially proud of this one: "The Butcher of Cambodia is at the dinner parties spooning up the sorbet." I read it to my editor on the telephone. As I start the assignment, Kissinger and I walk together through the Boston Commons, passing swan boats. I am huge. He takes my elbow at the curb. "I am worried that you might deliver right here," he says.

He sits me down and says, "Before we start this interview, we have to have an agreement. I will be able to change my quotes and edit every word I say."

He sees my shock. He knows and I know this violates every journalism rule.

That is the agreement I have with *The New York Times* and *The Washington Post*, he says coolly.

This turns out to be a lie.

I stammer: If that is the agreement they have with you, okay. It's lame, but I am new to the big lie game.

I do not change anything.

And now he is screaming on the phone just before I go into labor. My mother answers it when he calls. "Your daughter called me a manipulator!" he screams.

"Dr. Kissinger, I am so sorry," my mother says.

"Why did you say that?" I yell.

"He's famous," she says.

Ninety-six hours later, Casey has arrived.

Champagne waits in the hospital room.

At the bottom of the glass, a diamond, twinkling.

At that moment in my young life, the luck card. I have no illusions about that.

4 8

Nighttime. I pretend to Carl that I am exhausted and hug him as we pull into the motel. He's getting thinner, but not by much. He's eating huge amounts of food. He is fierce about his privacy. You haven't told anyone why you're here? Are you sure? I don't want anyone to know.

Tonight, at McGlinn's, a steak, red meat for the yang deficit Dr. Wong has convinced him that he has. I need it for the red blood count, he says, as he works his way through a ten-ounce sirloin. My thoughts are skittering this way and that, tangled in a huge knot of: I need to be in New York for my friend Annie who is coming down from Connecticut to the theater. I have to be in New York next week. I have to leave NOW. So much for all of the yoga, for all of the achieving of *sthira sukha*—the ideal Hindu balance of effort and ease. I can't exist in the nowness, this nowness. But the thought of holing up in an ashram to achieve the quieting of *vritti*, the mental chatter of my chronic monkey mind, makes me want to shoot myself. (I'm trying to learn not to say that.) So I am doing my version of that, zoning out with Larry King.

Carl's not in his room. I'm out in the hall in my sweats knocking on his door. He's taken the last copy of the *Times* sold at Starbucks and I want it back. Maybe if I see New York bylines, familiar names, places, the grid of events that is not being translated in the *Wenatchee World*, I can come back to myself, getting the voices to get out of my head, like this is your life, live in the now, chill out. I'm too much in myself, which is causing me to want to put my face in a quart of Jamoca Almond Fudge. How much time do Carl and I have left together? How can we reconcile? I want to be able to have a brother, to let him know that nothing matters that came before. All the words that are stuck there, in my throat, buried, incapable of getting out. What am I waiting for?

No one answers. That's unusual. He's usually up until ten. There's laughter coming from the swimming pool off the lobby. I walk down, expecting to find my brother in the small lobby, looking at the Internet.

No sign of Carl. But Bob is on the desk. "Are you looking for your brother? He just went out." It's almost ten o'clock in Wenatchee. Out on the driveway, I see his truck, pulling out of the parking lot, heading north.

Odd. Where could he be going at this hour?

Bob is one of those people who seem opaque, but he's got an instinct that something is amiss.

"He does that a lot. He just gets in the truck and takes off."

I decide I will wait in the lobby. To pass the time, I read and make notes on the local towns. How could I have been in Wenatchee all these weeks and not driven to Twisp, the sunflower capital of the state? "Whether you enjoy horseback riding, rafting, fishing, snowmobiling, cross-country or downhill skiing, dog sledding, hot air ballooning or just relaxing, Twisp is the place to be." I had missed everything: Waterville, "the highest elevated incorporated community in the state" at 2,600 feet with its Nifty Theatre and turn-of-the-century charm. I had missed

Mazama, not far from the North Cascades National Park, with its views of rock-climbing destinations of Liberty Bell and Early Winter Spires. Not to mention the Chief Joseph Dam, the Lake Roosevelt National Recreation Area, Fort Okanogan State Park. While I was immersed in my own fog, life and beauty were all around me, and I was here, fretting and trying to write in my journal, fighting the war within me. An hour passes, then another. I close my eyes and then Carl looms over me in the lobby. His face is stamped with worry lines, like I had gone crazy or something terrible had happened in New York. "What are you doing here?"

"Where were you?" I ask.

He looks away, angry and defensive. "Out driving. Just driving. Listening to *Parsifal*. What the hell difference does it make?"

Show me where you go, I say.

It's midnight, he says. We have to be at the packinghouse early.

I want to know, I say. Please, I say.

The only traffic on the road is the ten-wheelers from Wal-Mart and Dot Industries on their way to Canada. They blow us off the highway, commanding the lanes as Carl grips the wheel and makes that weird clenching sound in his teeth. The wind howls through the trees and the forest is a wall closing in on us. He's moving fast, like he's rushing toward something, away from something, on the highway that links Wenatchee and Chelan. At this hour, only the Arco Station is open, its sign flashing. I see that his speedometer is at 90 mph and we're on the Chelan road. The wooden frame farmhouses on the river are more forlorn than ever. The road narrows and we follow the water in the semidarkness, fireflies and stars in front of us.

"When was the last time you saw a firefly?" I ask.

The sounds of the arias fill the car, and we ride in silence into the long tunnel that opens up on the hills of Chelan. In the moonlight, the deserted orchards, soon to be burned, fade into the darkened sky, and the only lights come from the distant side of the lake. Carl circles past his orchard, through town, and then floors it on a narrow road on the north side of the lake.

Suddenly, Carl stops the car in front of an orchard that has just been pulled. Look at this, he says.

What?

Don't you see anything?

Just an empty field.

Look at the white marks, the chalk lines. They're marking it for a subdivision. Within a few years all of this property is going to be sold to real estate developers. Don't sell the land, he says. Hold on as long as you can. Keep them going, no matter what.

For once, I do not say anything, I just let him talk.

"Have you ever thought about how much energy is put into the negative—what is wrong with everyone and everything? This is a beautiful thing, growing fruit. You have no idea. . . . You don't know why I am here. I am here for a simple reason: It makes me happy. It makes me happy to grow fruit. I worry about you," he says. "I worry that it is hard for you to just let yourself be happy. To view your life as everything you have done right, not everything you have done wrong."

A few minutes pass in complete silence. Then: I am going to need oxygen tanks soon. Portable ones. It's no big deal. Don't start crying again. I could live a long time.

Then again: I don't want anyone to know. And that is my choice.

My stomach is in a tight ball, trying to take this in.

You're going to beat this, I say.

The numbers, he says. It's 11 percent.

Well, that means 11 percent make it.

He's suddenly irritated again. Stop spinning. Do you hear yourself?

He's twirling the radio dial until he finds all-night jazz coming from the university at Walla Walla.

Steppin' out with my baby
Can't go wrong, 'cause I'm in right
It's for sure, not for maybe
That I'm all dressed up tonight. . . .

There'll be smooth sailin' 'cause I'm trimmin' my sails
In my top hat and my white tie and my tails. . . .

Ask me when will the day be
The big day may be tonight

I look over to see tears running down Carl's cheeks. I hold his hand and put my feet on the dashboard. For once, my brother does not correct me.

You've built something beautiful here, I say.

Right, he says.

Night sounds. The birds in the trees, the sound of the trucks across 97A by the lake.

He grips the steering wheel hard and pulls back onto the road, his face cut with tension. We ride in silence for an hour, through the tunnels of Chelan, past the inky darkness of the Columbia River, finding our way into the motel at two a.m.

Well, good night, he says, all Carl-like and stiff again. I hope you can get some rest.

———

I told my friends: I'm moving to San Antonio. I may not be back for months.

Let me set down a few things that happened next.

1. I moved to a house that is in the same neighborhood where I grew up.

2. In a storage room somewhere near Bob's Barbeque and 410 Diner not far from the Austin Highway, I discovered all of the furniture that was in our childhood house.

3. Our house is reconstructed in a space that looks not so different from the very space in which Carl and I grew up.

When you land in San Antonio, the first view is of trees that seem to stretch all the way north to the Texas hill country. Sometimes in the spring, you can see bluebonnets from the air.

I was frightened to go back.

My mother's friend Louise is a wise and loving observer of everyone's foibles, with a tenderness that draws the world to her, no matter what. "I've passed a cute house with a FOR RENT sign. Let me take a look. Maybe we can get you moved in before Thanksgiving," she said. "Just send me the key to the storage room."

"I can just feel your mother in these rooms," Louise said on the day I arrived. Carl walked in the door to see the tables with ball-and-claw legs, the antique clocks, and the Japanese prints that had been our setting. He immediately walked into the kitchen to check out what was in the refrigerator. "You are probably expecting to see some of Thelma's mango mold there," Louise said. "Yeah," he said.

We were moving through uncharted terrain, our customs as remote as if we had grown up in separate tribes.

In fact, we had. Within the family, there were two clubs: father-son and mother-daughter. Carl and I could never work out the reasons why.

"My work was Carl, and Thelma's, Marie," my father said to explain our divided vacations, our dinners that were conducted as if for Balkan nations, and the boys-against-girls atmosphere that pervaded the house and became a joke. But was that reality, or a mystery locked within attachment, not given to easy answers? "Am meeting Carl for lunch," my mother wrote me frequently, in her letters. Or: "I am taking Carl's girlfriend Jan shopping. We're doing a makeover! I like her a lot," she wrote about a young reporter Carl dated in his twenties. When they broke up, the tone of her letters changed: "Please find someone great for Carl. He's a catch!" He brooded about what he perceived was her sense of his life.

"She wants me to be in the real estate business with all those crooks," he said once in an angry telephone call. "I told her, 'Is that what you care about?'" "Why do you care what she thinks?" I asked him then. "It's your life."

He drew in on himself in a zone of silence that no one could penetrate.

We were soon playing out the roles assigned to us: Carl as dominating older brother; Marie as flighty and rebellious younger sister. We arranged to meet at Star Storage on Broadway and go through boxes from our parents' house. I followed Carl down the long hallways of the storage center and watched him as he opened the first room, a room I had not seen. There, meticulously labeled, were box after box. Hundreds of cartons. Their labels noted: "Kitchen Pots and Pans"; "Tea Towels"; "Video Tapes."

"I thought you gave all this away," I said. "It's junk."

"It's not," he said. "These things are valuable."

"Tea towels? Videos? No one even uses videos anymore."

On top of a video box were two tapes our mother had bought for him at the Metropolitan Museum of Art.

"Do you remember the fight you had over these?" I said.

"What are you talking about?"

"Mother got these for your birthday—van Gogh and Gauguin. You accused her of regifting and giving you old tapes. They cost twenty-five dollars then!"

"You're making this up," he said.

That argument between them had occupied days of conversation. She was in New York, being treated for cancer, and would go to the Met to hear the lectures, then pick up Casey at summer day camp across the street. In her last good months, Carl was furious with her, playing out some inner drama in his head. "Whatever I do, I am wrong," she said often that summer. "He is angry with me all the time. Why is he so angry?"

"Mother loved you, Carl," I said quietly. "You were horrible to her when she was sick."

He didn't answer.

I continued looking in the box. It was filled with family pictures. Then, at the bottom, there was a file of receipts. In the file, there was a receipt from the Met's gift shop. "Look," I said. "The evidence. She bought the tapes. They weren't used."

"What's your point?" he said.

"You never saw her," I said. "You could not take it in. You do not want to take in another version. Anger gives you power."

"Is this what your psychiatrist says?"

The ghosts danced around us, their shadows distortions on the walls.

———

Carl lived in a large stone house, a family house tucked behind a fine French restaurant, not far from where we grew up.

"I must say with annoyance that you have done an excellent job decorating here," I said. There were zebra skin rugs downstairs, lion skins upstairs, Victorian buffets, and the walls were hung with paintings of apples and old prints. Opera was piped all over the house.

We are speeding toward La Fonda for our ritual welcome-home dinner of soft chicken tacos and *salsa verde*, corn tortillas freshly made. We are greeted by Alicia in her embroidered shirt, who has known us all these years.

Home.

He is at his best, custodial and careful. I was often quiet around him, quieter than with anyone else in my life, withdrawn into a place behind a wall as if it was difficult to speak.

As always, we know many people in the room. Soon I am up, saying hello to friends I have not seen in months.

Are you running for mayor? Carl says when I sit down. I finished your guacamole for you. I hope you don't mind.

And then it all begins again, the way it's always been.

Do you know what Bounce is?

Of course I know what Bounce is.

What is it?

You put it in the dryer to make your clothes soft.

Do you know what color the box is?

Are you insane?

Do you think you could go to the Wal-Mart and get me a box? Take this box with you, just in case you forget. You might forget what it looks like. You know how you are. It is important you not make a mistake.

He looks at me, and in his face I see my own, the same mysterious gaze.

"Don't touch anything in these boxes," Carl says.

"How can you have so many boxes cluttering up your living room? They are an eyesore. I will clean them out for you," I say.

No, he says. *I don't want anyone touching anything.*

This is ridiculous. These boxes in a living room look like the Collyer Brothers.

The discussion is over, he says. *People just give me things. I never know what to do with them. So I just put them in the boxes.*

Carl's house is large enough for a family of five, with an upstairs sitting room and extra bedrooms, one of which has been turned into an office. There's a cheerful kitchen with sky blue cabinets and antique cupboards of gleaming porcelain. In the hall is an art deco built-in china cabinet with glass doors. There is so much china he could have dinners for fifty every night.

I follow my brother through a TV room adjoining the living room. A large antique safe takes up an entire wall. It's from the original Solo Serve and the date—1915—is painted on the side.

The door is open. There are guns, shotguns and pistols and ammunition.

I am giving all of them to Aubrey, he says, mentioning a cousin who likes to hunt.

But not the pistol, he says. The pistol I am keeping.

I don't register the remark.

"When are you coming home?" Ernie asked me every few days on the telephone. *I am home,* I thought. *I have never left. I am where I have always been.*

"I want you to learn to make a pie," Carl said just before Thanksgiving. "Heather has agreed to teach you. She is going to give you a cooking lesson."

We were meeting at Central Market for lunch. It was the Alamo Heights haven, the place where you see everyone you know and have known your entire life. I had my bike chained outside and had made the thrilling discovery that Central Market now sold the *New York Post*. It came two days late and cost $3, but it was a lifeline in the Sahara, what a shrink would call a soteria, a linking object to the past.

Somehow I had taken this time to be in the present, not the past. I was struggling with all of these implications, falling down a chute.

"I thought you were in love with Allegra," I said. "Isn't she on her way for Thanksgiving?"

"Yes," he said, suddenly brusque. "And you are to let Allegra be the star at Thanksgiving. Allegra is making poached pears for dessert."

"Who is making pumpkin pie? I'll pick up one."

"We are not having pumpkin pie. Nothing store-bought. You and Heather are making an apple pie. With my Braeburns. And something else, there is no turkey this year. I am cooking a goose. I shot it special."

"You did that when mother was dying. It was disgusting. The house smelled like burning fat."

"You're crazy," he said. "It was delicious. Mother loved it."

"She did not eat a single bit of it. She died four days later. There was buckshot in it."

"Well, Daddy liked it."

"Casey and James are flying from college across the country and they can't have turkey and a pumpkin pie but have to eat prissy poached fucking pears?"

"You always want everything your way."

An hour later, my cell phone rings.

"Your brother has called me. He's wild about the turkey. He says you are not allowed to have a turkey." Ernie, from the office, trying not to sound amused.

"I don't think this is funny. I want a turkey. Casey and James are not flying across the country to eat some hideous goose."

I am sorry to report that for the next thirty-six hours, there are eight phone calls on the subject of the Thanksgiving turkey.

Okay, I lost.

There was no turkey at the Thanksgiving dinner of 2002.

There was, however, a pumpkin pie.

49

A miracle.

The Reverend Ilene Brenner Dunn was in her office when she saw the red light flashing on the answering machine. "This is Carl Brenner," a voice said. "You may not remember me, but I hear you are back in town. I don't think we have seen each other since you were in college. My sister, Marie, is an author and is coming to town for a speech. Would you like to come?"

He had been on his way to play basketball in the King William district when he noticed a sign under the glass on the front of Madison Square Presbyterian Church:

THIS SUNDAY: DIRTY LIVING

MATTHEW 13

THE REVEREND ILENE BRENNER DUNN

Carl slowed his car down and stared at the small marquee. *Ilene Brenner Dunn.* He stopped short and said out loud, "Holy shit."

The church bordered a historic park in downtown San Antonio, a few blocks from the Alamo. *Ilene.* He hadn't thought about her for years. She was close to his own age, one of three sisters, the oldest daughter of our grandfather Isidor's second marriage. Aunt Ilene. Our half aunt.

Ilene was startled, then delighted by his call. She had recently moved back to San Antonio from her church in Austin. We had known her and her sisters, Becky and Leslie, when we were children, but they drifted out of our lives, vanished into the ether of the Brenner wars. Now Ilene, at the age of fifty-seven, had brought her reputation as a firebrand activist to Madison Square Presbyterian Church.

Carl sounded elated when he called; light, even. "You are not going to believe this. Ilene is back in town."

Ilene played the message several times. *Carl.* Her first emotion on hearing his voice was the purest happiness, an excitement that a missing puzzle-piece in her life had surfaced, just like that. She had a vivid memory of him as a six-year-old, stomping on her dolls, making a lot of boy noise in the pool. He'd been in high school the last time she had seen him. He sounded just like Milton. Commanding, but there was something yearning underneath his voice, unsure of the reception he would get. She was used to that voice with all of her parishioners. The voice of looking for answers. She did not want to read too much into a simple message. *This will be fascinating,* she told her sister Becky, who lived in Seattle. The Brenner kids again.

For months, tension had been rocking her congregation. Ilene, who lived in Washington, D.C., and Austin, was trying to hold steady against the influence of the archconservatives who were threatening her beloved Presbyterian Church. Madison Square had a long, proud history of activist politics, all the way back to 1874. Suffragettes and civil rights activists; yellow dog Texas

Democrats. Ilene shared the same passions, and was quietly promoting gays and lesbians, some of them from Fort Sam Houston, as church elders, against the new rules of her church. She made no secret of her feelings. *You are such a Brenner,* I said the first time we saw each other. *You have the Milton DNA.*

I stand up for what I believe, she said.

How odd, she later thought, that Carl had reached out to her when he did. On the day she got the telephone call from the nephew she had not seen in forty years, she was working on a sermon about dirt. The sign was in the front of the church when he drove by. THIS SUNDAY: DIRTY LIVING.

There were certainly parables that were better-known, like those of the Prodigal Son and the wedding banquet, but Jesus' belief that man was made up of all kinds of soil—thorny, fertile, sandy, rocky—was Ilene's favorite. On the lectionary calendar, it came in March, when the bluebonnets hit the hill country. The parable was from Matthew 13. This year she was writing about her friend Mary Ann Moses, out planting trees near Marfa, Texas, where the plains had been colonized by contemporary artists like Donald Judd. Marfa was known for its rocky soil. Nothing less than a jackhammer could break through it.

Then Carl. On the wall of her office, near her diplomas from the seminary, she kept a picture of her father and mother at the time they were married. Her mother, Rita, had been her father's secretary. Isidor was sixty-eight when they married, and Rita, twenty-eight. The marriage scandalized the families of Temple Beth-El in 1941 as all their sons were leaving for the war. Isidor was too much of a maverick to care what any of them thought; it was a love match that endured. Rita, a petite beauty with size 3 feet, was from a French family in Louisiana. The youngest of nine children, she had lost both her parents by the time she was thirteen. She started as a clerk at Solo Serve and impressed the

boss with her style, her love of beautiful clothes, and her lilting
New Orleans tone. She was promoted to be his secretary, and soon
they were out dancing three times a week. Furious letters went
back and forth between Brenner siblings, but Rita was Isidor's passion, and he left one life for a happier, more carefree one.

Now he rode through San Antonio in a convertible with his
bride-to-be, scandalizing everyone who knew him as a staunch
reader of the Torah at Beth-El. Soon after Pearl Harbor, he
stopped speaking to his youngest son, Milton, who was outraged
by the marriage, calling him a worthless son-of-a-bitch for aban-
doning his mother. Milton was already a captain in the army, running the finances for a base in the Rio Grande Valley. He had
come up with an ingenious way to save the army millions of dollars on expenses and had caught the attention of Washington,
D.C. The new Air Transport Command sought his advice on
hires for finance. "I can do this job," he said from Harlingen, in
the Rio Grande Valley. The call had taken hours to come
through, involving two different military operators.

"How old are you, Captain?"

"Twenty-nine," he said.

"Are you a Jew?"

A pause. "Yes, sir."

"Well, the boss, C. R. Smith, doesn't take to Jews. And you
have to be a colonel."

"I'm not like other Jews. I'm from Texas," he said. "And Mexico. You can promote me. Make me a Lieutenant Colonel."

He blazed to the top of the Air Transport Command, but he
did not receive a letter from Isidor until the end of the war, when
he commended him on his service and asked him to come home to
help him run the stores.

Ilene did not meet her brother until she was five. He was thirty-four years old and had brought his new bride back to San Antonio. They drove out to the big house on Morningside Drive and watched Ilene and her baby sisters splash in the pool. Each Friday night, Ilene rode in the convertible to Temple Beth-El with her father and memorized portions of the Torah at the Sunday school. Her Jewish education never left her, and she was careful never to preach miracle healings or allow her parishioners to think floods and transformations were anything more than useful myths.

After Carl and I were born, she was occasionally our babysitter. Soon after her father died, the family erupted into a long battle over his will. Rita went on to more marriages. Ilene's stepfathers were devout Baptists, and anything that seemed Jewish was forbidden.

Ilene and her sisters, and Aunt Anita, Uncle Henry, and Aunt Leah, evaporated from our lives, as if we had dreamed that they were real.

5 0

You don't have to be Freud to understand that brothers and sisters have a huge effect on each other. The fact that psychiatry more or less ignored this for eighty years would be enough reason never to talk to a therapist again. As I write this, I realize that this perception is pure Carl. I am becoming more like Carl than I ever dreamed.

Jung had a theory about brothers and sisters—that they were much more powerful than anyone had ever thought. That siblings stayed in each other's life through the corridors of time, and that not studying them, downplaying their influence on one another has been one of the great unexplained gaps of psychoanalytic theory. Freud famously detailed sibling rivalries in two early cases, known by students of Psychology 101 as the Rat Man and the Wolf Man, but he did not focus on the effect of brothers and sisters on each other. He was the doted-upon firstborn, and many Freudian scholars cite his status as the family favorite as the reason he downplayed the effect of siblings on personality. Drumming his theories of sexual rivalries, murderous intentions toward the parents, sexual inadequacies, Freud ignored the basic fact that by age eleven, siblings devote one-third of their time to each other, far more than they spend with friends, with their parents, or even by themselves. Had Freud just not turned his attention to this aspect of personality? Now an entire new field of sibling study has opened up, and family therapists use the model of siblings and their problems with each other to predict what can be expected in a marriage.

I arrange to see a psychiatrist named Justin Frank. Frank practices in Washington and has turned out a smart, nutty book about George W. Bush called *Bush on the Couch*, in which he spends a chapter or two analyzing Bush's anger at a younger sister who died of cancer when he was seven. Frank believes that you can understand the entire later history of George W. and the war if you can understand that Bush had the older-brother syndrome of anger at the younger child, then what he calls "unresolved guilt issues" when she dies of cancer and his parents whisk the matter away as if it never happened. He uses terms like "dissociation" and "splitting," which mean largely that you lose who you are in order not to feel your rage, guilt, or pleasure at the loss.

I think that's what it means.

I know he has spent much time thinking about siblings, so I'm hoping he can point me in some direction that will get my cloud bank to lift. It's not a session but an interview. I'm trying to master the material through the back door of interviewing, hoping that his research will be a key in the lock.

I've booked a table at an elegant downtown restaurant. When I arrive, he says, "They had one table for us, but it was not quiet enough." I say, "Oh, I booked a table as well." I notice a shadow pass over his face, just a flicker, as if somehow it was not okay for me to have asserted that I too had made a call.

We sit down to order. Frank wears a purple shirt. He is often mistaken for the TV movie critic Gene Shalit. He has a handlebar mustache, an unusually shmoozy personality. Theories fly through the air and he is not afraid just to get it out there, what he thinks. "A lot of people in my profession do that hiding thing," he tells me. "I don't believe in it."

On the telephone, Frank used a term with me, "the Humpty Dumpty syndrome." That one is simple: The firstborn who feels that the younger sibling has pushed him or her off the wall. It cannot be that simple, I say.

You would be surprised, he says.

"Truth number one: How you are with your sibling has nothing to do with how you are out in the world," Frank says.

I had asked him a single question: Why is it impossible for many to view their siblings in the way their siblings present to their friends? In other words, how can I not see that my brother, a furious jerk with me, was, for his friends, a deeply loyal, charming apple man, opera lover, and wine buff. What was wrong with me?

Frank uses a case study that comes from the beliefs of the psychoanalyst Melanie Klein. "The first rival for a baby's attention is actually the mother's mind," he says. "Have you ever noticed a baby yanking on a telephone cord to get the mother to pay attention? You want to have your mother's complete attention. And then when a new baby comes, the attention is shattered in an entirely different way."

At Harvard Medical School, Frank had a teacher he called the Malignant Marshmallow. He was a father figure, Frank recalled, very tough and very soft. "We vied for his attention. It would drive me crazy when one of my classmates would say, X actually prefers me. I knew that I was the one that Professor X preferred."

He would spend hours obsessing about this and took it to his own psychiatrist. "At the time I was aware in my own therapy of my younger sister Ellen. And how guilty I felt and how difficult it was for me to accept her, how angry I was that she existed."

I play to Frank, praise him in a way that I use with my brother. It's like I am inhabited by an incubus. My wall of falseness has come up and I am hiding behind a façade. I leave the table feeling flattened and uncomfortable, as if I have ceased to exist. I fall into the classic younger sister mode with a self-absorbed older brother. It is an automatic response. On the surface, we have a fascinating conversation and I learn a lot. He is generous to spend time with me and generous with his insights. So what is wrong with me? Why am I so angry? What am I bringing to this encounter?

I walk out with the beginning of a theory that maybe Justin Frank is wrong, at least in my case. How you are with your siblings is directly related to how you are in the world. And that I have one view of my brother, locked in place about the time he set me sailing out the window near my crib.

Sibling transference.

I understand the term for the first time in London, in a small house in Wandsworth near the village green.

Let me set the scene:

The reception room of Prophecy Coles, a delicate woman in a long tweed skirt. She greets me in a cozy library with faded William Morris wallpaper that looks like it belongs to a Cambridge don. I had discovered a monograph she had written: *The Importance of Sibling Relationships in Psychoanalysis*. The question I have set myself now to answer is how writing about my father and his brother and sisters and my own life with Carl is setting off in me what feels like an elevator crashing to the bottom, as if I have no safety net. I have Coles's address scrawled on a notebook sheet along with some start-up questions: What led her to it? How did she break down the research tactics and topics? What breakthroughs have come up in sibling research? What was her own relationship with her siblings?

Coles, close to her older brother, was the second of four children in a Dorset family of post-Bloomsbury intellectuals. She plunged into the jungle of the new sibling theorists because of a patient she had.

She calls her Mrs. K.

Mrs. K appeared in Wandsworth, same traffic jam, same tube stop, but with overwhelming problems she was having with a sister.

Mrs. K appeared in the office of Prophecy Coles with an ongoing problem. She despised her sister, and the feeling was mutual. They were locked in some mutually satisfying toxic hate bond. Mrs. K ignored her first psychiatrist, who suggested she dash off a poisonous letter, a kiss-off, and never speak to her sister again. She rejected that advice, ditched the doctor, and found Coles in Wandsworth. For months they got nowhere. Until Coles, close to her older brother, suddenly put the lens on her own complicated life. Eureka! Her younger sister was her bête noire; Coles was playing this out through Mrs. K.

What the case of Mrs. K tells me is a version of what I heard at a sibling conference held at Adelphi University in May 2007. A *Time* cover suggested that our siblings are the dark matter that pulls at us, but there is much confusion on the issue. It's fashionable at sibling conferences to pull out the much-quoted early research of Alice Colonna and Lottie Newman, who reported in 1983 that "siblings are not mentioned in the standard psychiatrist tests." But since then there has been a geyser of theories, books, and assertions. Couples therapists pose questions at forums with giddy abandon: Was competitive neurotic behavior rooted in all siblings? Francine Klagsbrun argued in *Mixed Feelings: Love, Hate, Rivalry, and Reconciliation Among Brothers and Sisters* that "buried sibling images"—positive and negative—can have a greater impact on behavior than parents. Here is Boston psychologist Dr. Jody Leader, presenting a paper on the same subject:

"Sibling relationships impact one's own deepest sense of self. They provide rich opportunities for mutual learning. . . . It is through sibling relationships that the first understanding of group feelings is defined as well as the first stirrings of justice."

Again from Jody Leader:

"These early relationships deeply influence each level of intimacy as well as the distinct style of communication as the kind of defenses they employ. . . . When these sibling relationships are conflict based and unresolved, there is a compulsion to repeat."

In other words, the Bermuda triangle that can never be explained but allows you to experience colleagues and partners with something approaching the mind-set you had with your siblings. Did you look to them as mentors, enemies, confidants, or competitors? Or a combination of all of these elements, depending on the day?

Now that I understood it, that it was there, underneath, like a cop directing the traffic, it would take every shred of discipline to look for the common ground, the links that attached us to the world rather than the thing that separated us. And that was a decision, like choosing chocolate over strawberry, that was within me to make.

I failed at this much of the time.

In San Antonio, I lay out copies of the letters from the Harry Ransom archive on the dining room table in my house. They drift over the chairs in unwieldy piles. The Brenners took exquisite notice of each other's needs—job searches, dress buys, who was coming into town for parties.

I have discovered Rosebud, I tell Carl, drenched in pride.

That's nice, he says, and walks out of the room.

He now keeps a card by his bed:

Celtic Prayer (practice each morning)

God who gave me life,
Preserve my life today.
Lord Christ who redeemed my life,
Purify my soul today.
Holy Spirit, Life Companion,
Walk the path with me today.
(Amen)

Think of it, I tell Carl.

Daddy, at twenty-one, learns his father has been having a long affair with one of the Solo Serve cashiers. He hires a private detective, confronts him in a small conference room, and takes after him with a riding quirt. Isidor calls the San Antonio sheriff and has his son arrested, which makes the local papers. He tells him: *You are out of this family. And I mean forever.*

Roosevelt is running for president. Anita, at twenty-seven, in New York, is contributing regularly to *The New York Times* and is the art critic of *The Nation.* The store is almost bankrupt. She writes her idiot younger brother:

Sept 1, 1932:
Dear Milton,
. . . I am unquestionably shocked at your attitude, and surprised, too; because I was under the impression that you would act with your head, instead of with your impulses. After all, people just don't go about hitting their fathers, no matter what the provocation; it is hardly the admirable thing to do, and I am more ready to take my hat off to the man who, in like circumstances, gets hit but doesn't hit back. You are hitting a man who is not physically your equal, and who is also entitled to your respect, at least for your debts to him. . . .

. . . You have been playing the part of the famous bull in the china shop. . . .

. . . It is not going to help Mama any, to drag her through the dirt and indignity of a divorce trial. Furthermore, she cannot stand it physically and will be a complete wreck if it is forced upon her. . . .

Next, yourself. It is natural that Papa should wish to never see you again, and, given your attitude of—"If they don't do as I ask, it means war!"—it is natural that he should wish to punish you, and carry it as far as the courts, and the rest of it. But just, what is the point? What are you defending, and who are you fighting, but yourself, throughout? Don't you see that you are laying the fuse for a tremendous bomb, the results of which no one can foresee, and which will involve all of us? Can't you give us a chance to ask you not to do that—to swallow your pride, as we have all done, each in our time for a little peace? . . .

Well. So endeth my sermon. If my so-called prestige as a writer is worth a damn, it will accomplish perhaps, in part, what seems to be painfully urgent; and the whole thing in a nutshell is simply a very urgent plea to you, begging you not to carry out your ideas and policy as planned. And if you can't make up your mind, for God's sake, I mean God!—don't do anything at all. . . .

But, please, write me. And wire if anything new happens.

Much love from Anita

I try to imagine my father, at twenty-one, with what would feel to him like a grenade lobbed down to Texas from the Famous One. In fact, everything Anita said was perfectly reasonable, sisterly concern from any sister's point of view. *This is nonsense,* Carl says, when I tell him about it later.

I can feel our father ball up the letter, throw it across the room, get on the typewriter, and start banging out lengthy defenses layered with contemptuous remarks. Thinking better of it. Talking to his mother, being talked out of his bull in the china shop. The world is falling apart, his father has mortgaged the stores to the hilt. In New York, there are Hoovervilles in Central Park, and Anita worries that her younger brother's temper will cut off any hope of an income stream. She surely imagined her father pulling the carpet on anyone who wasn't on his team. She's newly married, scrambling on a Guggenheim fellowship, her handsome husband, David Glusker, treating patients for free, to build a practice. And now Milton, acting out.

Write it in a play, my brother says, snorting. *You'll make it up anyway.*

Too much reality makes you uncomfortable, I say.

That's bullshit, Carl says.

In San Antonio, the Mexicans who shell pecans will soon go out on strike, setting off fires and weeks of violence not so far from town. Don Isidor, locked in a marriage that was surely dead, an alliance of children and loyalties and an understanding of their pasts, searched for colors, to feel alive again.

Why could no one understand?

Anita came the closest. The favorite daughter.

She might have mailed her father a carbon copy. I have no proof of that. But it would be an act of a firstborn, a gotcha that anyone could understand. She was good at that. And then kept it all in the files.

She was by then a young superstar, at her best in her years as a correspondent for *The New York Times Magazine*. Her dispatches sometimes made page one—the news of an oil concession given to the president of Mexico—but she was most known for her prescient understanding of the vogue for all things Mexican. Some critics dismissed her as an apologist for the muralists, but she was given a plum assignment: to sail to Paris to interview

Trotsky in exile. Greatness and conspiracy, adoring followers and conniving plotters surrounded the revolutionary disenfranchised Russian ruler. She wrote: "I was told to write this Mr. X., care of Poste Restante, in a city in France."

I am writing about this in detail because, even now, the miracle of an aunt being the reporter dispatched to interview the leader of a fallen Russia fills me with nothing short of wonder.

After several weeks of waiting in Paris for Trotsky to respond, she recounted:

"A brief note arrived telling me to write to another address. . . . In Paris, a voice on the telephone set a rendez-vous in a café, asking me to identify myself in a certain way." She was told that an interview would be difficult to arrange: "'White Russians . . . terrorists . . . royalists . . . Fascists . . . and secret agents of many sorts would have their own reasons wanting to get at him.'" At a third meeting with Trotsky's men, she wrote that one told her, "Let us go." Where? "'Somewhere in France.' And I went in a closed car at night, dutifully making every effort not to look through the shutters of the car . . . carefully trying not to notice how long it was taking me to get there."

Her initial impression of Trotsky was that he was "a cold, shy, harassed man," and she was put off by his steely gaze, "with a sharp light in [his eyes] that I have seen only twice before, once in the face of an artist and once, an explorer." She was pleased that he turned out to be a cheerful man, with "lifts of gaiety."

Looking at it now, the writing seems thin; shallow, even—*lifts of gaiety?*

Anita was also instrumental in arranging his eventual Mexican asylum by cabling Rivera. The telegram has been lost to history, but family lore says it read, "Uncle is sick and would like a Mexican holiday." Rivera prevailed on Mexican president Lázaro Cárdenas to allow Trotsky into the country, where he lived in the now famous house in the Coyoacán district of Mexico City surrounded by loyalists, tended rabbits and chickens, and had an affair with Frida Kahlo.

Soon after, Anita wrote a telling letter to Kahlo, who was considering remarrying the faithless Rivera: "Don't let yourself be tied down completely, do something with your own life, for that is what cushions us when the blows and the falls come. . . . One depends only on oneself, and from there must come everything." How prophetic. Within the decade, her own marriage would collapse and she would be consumed with trying to put out her magazine *Mexico/This Month*, convinced that the FBI had amassed a dossier on her political connections.

51

I've spent years imitating Carl, using him as comic material, running away from his telephone calls.

La señora no está.

Now I am all he has.

Now he is my safety net and I am his.

I am going to spin out here. Nothing will be left of me. By the time this is over, I will not have a career. I will be in Wenatchee, thirty pounds fatter, living on Krispy Kremes. I am losing my story. I cry on the telephone to my husband. He sounds frustrated, shut down in silence. Let me call you back, he says.

Have I married Carl too?

I blank out here. A psychiatrist calls this "a rage reaction." I can suddenly think only about Aunt Dorothy in her fifties, complaining in Mexico City about her maid, Dorlia. "She is so willful." Her lover comes in the afternoon and Dorlia serves him the Mexico City lunch, the grand meal of the day. They have the satisfying relationship of seeing each other only in the afternoons and traveling together in the summers, hitting the high spots in

Arles, sitting outdoors in cafés taking a high dive into their evening clarets, determined to be seen.

The threads of the tapestry sewn in their twenties eroded their relationships. Dorothy and Milton allied against Anita and Henry and Leah, and it was impossible for me not to assume that everything that happened in their lives could be seen like a distant warning in these long farragoes of emotions hurling back and forth and kept by Anita in her files in Mexico City.

Why did she preserve them with such care?

Was Anita longing for a connection with her lost brother and sister as they yearned for her? Here it is, Your Honor, the discovery material. Check out my side of the case. *Hear me out.*

Anita, like Carl, was drawn to the land. Her last years were spent farming white asparagus in Aguascalientes, at the family ranch. The records of her efforts are at the archive as well.

I am trying, again, to get used to Carl.

Let's join hands before we plate down, he says.

"Father Jesus," he says before every meal. I tell Casey about it on the telephone. "This is impossible," she says. "Thank God Nana is not alive." I suddenly remember my grandfather's tefillin in her drawer.

Where do you get your bravery? I ask him. The moon is high in the sky. It is clearly not a question to ask of a spiritual man. "What is my suffering compared to Jesus?" he says. "Christ had his arms and legs nailed to the cross. My suffering is nothing compared to that. It is a tragedy that you don't have spiritualism in your life."

A few days later, he asks me to have my blood taken. "I want to see the results," he says. "You know you could have something wrong. Everyone dies. You've had cancer. You could have it back again. You better get that blood test. The CEA. It's a cancer marker. And I want to check the levels myself when you see them. Don't trust what the doctor says."

In the basement, I find a box and a diary. It is marked in red, scenes and moments of my life in my twenties when the first real work began. I was struggling in London. I did this and that.

You could make a case that everything in this diary is a predictor of everything else, like a genetic marker; that what happened there had a ripple effect. But that would not explain the fact that it will take me twenty-five years to get to India but that I will and it will transform my life. It will not explain that the Supreme Court rules that women can be in a locker room and that means that I am lucky enough to get to travel with the Red Sox and it is how I meet the father of my daughter, the child who becomes the only true love and constant in my life. It does not explain the love that suddenly makes you think, But I have a daughter who is out there in the world, beautiful and brave, and I did that well, and this is where she lived and climbed in and out of the gardens up and down the block and had playdates and was upset when her friend Alex Leo had the cake with the Cinderellas and she had one with only strawberries because her mother thought that was chic. The rush of children filled my life with their drenching happy noises, softball games, and everything sandwiches with roast beef and turkey and Swiss cheese, detective stories written in a Mead notebook by a nine-year-old who believed she was Harriet the Spy. I would look up from my glass office and see Casey in the tree of our tiny garden, hopping from wall to wall of the houses on East Eighty-fourth Street, and my heart would explode with a sense of, This is really happy. The house filled with kids, their tennis rackets, Rollerblades, lost Scrabble tiles, Nintendo sets. Casey learned to walk across York Avenue to her school on the East River at the age of nine, and it was impossible to believe that we lived in these blocks of the East Eighties just like anyone does in small-town America, everything within a five-block area: the library at East Seventy-ninth Street with its children's room that had not changed since *Eloise* was published in 1955; the sandwich shop near the park; the hot dog man who watched her grow up.

And it does not explain why Casey's backstory will be her own, except in the shadow of this grid of pools in Texas and grandparents who took her to zoos and doted on her and did not let her eat the candy that had the red dye #5 and told her always to put down toilet paper on public toilets no matter where she was. She will not have the apple gene in her direct DNA, but she will read memos of these orchards and get boxes from her uncle that will say on the card sent to Brown University, "These pears are special. I picked them myself. I went to a lot of trouble. Don't share them with your friends." "He is such a dork," she says, when the pears arrive, and to him, "Thank you, Uncle Carl, they are the best pears I have ever had." And to me, "How can you like him? He is impossible!" "He's my brother," I say. "This isn't about like."

52

Tight close-up: the lips of Cary Grant fill the screen. We're at *The Bishop's Wife*, a Cary Grant–Loretta Young black-and-white classic movie. It's a warm bath of kindness as a churlish priest played by David Niven tries to build a grand cathedral. Cary Grant is a suave, wisecracking angel attempting to push Niven into seeing what he is missing around him—his wife's heart, his child, his parishioners. It's a Christmas weeper with Loretta Young in her big house saying, "We used to be happy, Henry!" Grant, the Dr. Feelgood of the film, tosses out chestnuts like "We all come from our own little planets. That's why we're all different. That's what makes life interesting." Grant softens the meanies in Henry's parish, pushes Henry back to working for the poor, and brings love back into everyone's lives—except his own.

Carl and I sit next to each other in the dark, sharing a popcorn. How is it possible that we have never before been to a movie together? I ask my brother as we walk into the Stanford Theatre in downtown Palo Alto. The town is filled with Stanford kids on their bikes, dot-com millionaires on the verge of the bust. I've had to push Carl to come to the movies. Tomorrow he has a new procedure, an experimental treatment done at the Stanford University Medical Center that is painless and can take cancer tumors off his spine. He's determined to make his yearly fishing trip to Alaska, and part of that is an ongoing barrage of treatments using a new technique that zaps tumors without surgery—stereotactic radiotherapy. We've heard about it from a close friend who kept her brother going thirteen years by these methods, a stitch here, a stitch there, putting together our own crazy patchwork quilt of new trials and methods. When we come out of the movie, Carl is still bathed in the aura of Cary Grant and the bishop's quest. God sent me there, he said. He puts his arm around me and we walk to a local café. There he works his way through a large platter of hummus and two pieces of carrot cake. One has a birthday candle on it. I've bought him presents for his fishing trip. A new waterproof tackle vest, a fleece from Patagonia. Why did you spend the money? he asks. But he's secretly pleased and that makes me happy too.

I have spent the day at Genentech, a campus of labs and office buildings where the cutting-edge medicines are being developed. I've pushed my way in to talk to Gwen Fyfe, a scientist there, and learn for the first time about a new drug, Avastin, that is being tested on lung cancer patients. Trials for Avastin, which will go on to earn FDA approval in 2004, are well under way. There is no hope that Carl can get into one. Fyfe is elegant, petite, and friendly, with one of those smiles that crinkle her face.

Now we're on the way to Stanford. He will be in a special room, and in another, Dr. John Adler will use a computer to manipulate a robot that beams radiation at the hot spots on his spine. We drive in the allée of palms. I'm doing that thing, filling in the conversational airwaves with younger sister noise. "It's a pretty place to be treated, isn't it?" His face is cut with tension, thinking about the hours ahead. He's worried that he will be paralyzed. We walk past a chapel. "I want you to go in there during the procedure. Pray for me," he says.

A few days earlier, we're on our way to the Lark Creek Inn in Larkspur, Carl speeding up the highway. The oxygen tank rests on the floor, but so far he's not using it very much. Hold it carefully, he says. It's delicate. Let me drive, I say. No way, he says. You are the worst driver. Who taught you how?

You did.

That's bullshit.

Brad and Gail are late, and Carl is furious. Brad and Carl were fraternity brothers and have remained close friends. Before lunch we take a hike in the hills. Brad has a puppy's charm. In his house there is a glass case that has his frat paddle and baseballs sheathed in plastic. It's as if he's a teenager in a fifty-five-year-old's body, with the Northern California youthfulness still radiating.

All through the walk they're arguing about Saddam Hussein.

"Well, what are you going to do with him? We have to send twenty thousand troops in there."

Soon we're talking about Islam, the rise of Islam as a force, that it is not about Israel or the United States but something profound, something deep inside the religion from a thousand years back, that these conquerors will be out there like a many-headed Hydra and you can't just go in here, attacking without being provoked.

Carl and I are getting on each other's nerves. I am sick of his politics and his Carlness. It's pretty difficult to be fed up with a brother fighting cancer, but I am. I am tired of being the cheerleader, the mirror, the pasted-on role I have as new best friend. On the way to see Brad and Gail, we stop in Sausalito at the houseboat of a cousin we have not seen in some years. He has a Zen serenity, a Buddha in his living room. "Russell has an admirable ability to practice detachment and what is now called, annoyingly, mindfulness," I say.

Carl lashes out. "You have Russell all figured out, don't you?" Then, "You need to see a neurologist."

"Why?" I ask him, falling in.

"I've noticed that you are asking me questions and not realizing that you have asked them before. That could be an early sign of dementia. You know it runs in the family. Not Alzheimer's, but what Daddy got. The senile dementia."

He was eighty-eight, I say. I am fifty-one.

"Goddamn it," he says. "I think you have it early. All the signs are there."

We are back again in our bog, as if *The Bishop's Wife* had never happened, as if we have made no progress.

It's pretty hard to hate a guy with cancer in eight parts of his body, but I do. "You are a prick," I say. "You always have been and you always will be. Mother was right. Monster man."

"I'm sick," he says. "I'm not going to make it."

"I am not your lightning rod," I say.

We ride through the hills of Menlo Park, not speaking to each other, locked in the frozen zone that has inhabited us for most of our lives.

I stare out the window, wanting to jump out of the car.

We pull into the parking lot. "I have something to tell you. I didn't want to tell you before. Don't get out of the car. My CEA is wildly up. I had a new blood test. It's 21. The herbs are not working." He is screaming. "George Wong's herbs are not working! They're not working. I have faxed him the numbers and he has no answers. Nobody has any answers. There is cancer circulating all through my system."

Why didn't you tell me? I ask, as if my knowing would have changed anything.

I didn't want to upset you, he says. If the GVAX trial I am starting here doesn't work, that's it. I have no levers. There are no other options. That's it. Do you know what that means?

We will find something, I say.

No we won't, he says. All I can do is pray.

Don't say a word to Brad and Gail about my medical condition, he says. Brad gets panicky. I tried to talk to him this morning, but he gets into that childlike thing, like it's happening to him, not me.

We sit in an alcove with trees everywhere around us. Brad's wife, Gail, from England, soothes the conversation, moving it along with a tender deftness that only the English seem to have mastered.

Brad is one of those people who hide their agita with no dead-air space, the constant boosting himself up, the résumé shuffling that is waving out there, hey, I'm hanging in, look at all the wonderful things I am doing! I know why he is doing this; it's killing him to see a close friend fighting out the endgame, but is the most empathic subject he can raise the news of their new house in Sea Ranch, two and a half hours away?

I am guilty of this too. So I really hate it when I see what I do in others.

We are in a split-screen reality, listening to the good news from the world of the well, with their opaque flag waving fair weather, we are so lucky, smug sense of entitlement, all the while not understanding that they are talking to someone whose time is on the clock, waiting to hear if his lymph nodes will get him a place in the GVAX trial.

Seeing Carl, Brad panics. He cannot let any airspace into the conversation:

We've put a bid on one in the middle of the redwoods! It's a place where our grandchildren can come! A place to have my brother come and our families! Lucky us!

This is how people talk in the world of the well.

I am ready to jump across the table and pull his tongue out of his throat.

I watch Carl's face listening to Brad's travel plans. I exist and soon you won't. Another baby boomer losing leverage, grasping at the vines.

After lunch we take a hike in the nearby hills. Carl leaves his oxygen in the car. I don't need that, he says, pumped up and alpha. He walks briskly ahead of all of us. Brad shakes his head. He always has to do stuff like this, he says. That's why we called him Man Mountain. The hills are covered with the wildflowers of June, the clumps of laurel and sunflowers, the buttercups that make us feel like we are walking through a golden cloud. There's a clump of houses on the hills being built. "Those go for at least a million, probably two," Brad says.

It hasn't rained in a while and the grass is dry and patchy. We talk about that too.

Suddenly, I look up to see Carl racing down a hill toward a chinning bar, running as fast as he did when he ran track. Carl, goddamn it! Brad sprints after him, puffing, in a turquoise cap. From a distance, I see my brother chinning on the bar, his muscles rippling under a white Lacoste shirt. He pulls himself up, twenty perfect chin-ups.

He's laughing when he jumps down with the Carl look of "fuck you" on his face, fuck the cancer and fuck dying and I will show you. Then he sees his shirt, covered with red blood.

We run, panic, scream: CARL!

"It's nothing," he says. "I just popped a few stitches. They had to cut me yesterday for a test. They took out a lymph gland and stitched me up. It's nothing. Anyone can stitch me up again."

"I'm not dead yet," he says, happy with himself.

We walk back in silence.

"You are acting like an idiot," I say, furious.

Casey arrives in Palo Alto. This is a good thing because I am in big trouble in Carl Land. She's called me with a drama, a hiccup in a romance with her college boyfriend, now panicky about leaving for a semester abroad. "When are you coming home?" she says. "Our whole life has become Uncle Carl. What is this?" I convince her to get on a plane, come join us in Palo Alto, be in the soothing redwood forests. Soon I am on the bridge to Oakland to pick her up at JetBlue. She's a whirl of a life force, at nineteen, a tumble of energy, cascading dark hair. Her arrival lets me unrev, be carried in her energy out of the pool of sadness and aloneness.

On her first morning in Palo Alto, exhausted from her finals, her uncle bombards her with his plans for her. "I want you to go to Cornell Agricultural School after college," he says. "You need to learn how to be a farmer. And most of all there is one lesson that is the most important. You have to learn to dig in the dirt. That's what running orchards is about. How to dig."

He's all keyed up this morning, flying on steroids and the meds he was pumped with when he had his stitches repaired. He's rushing past me through the roses of the Stanford gardens, the honey-colored buildings. I'm six inches shorter and in moccasins, struggling to keep up with his loping stride.

"Are you there? Why are you so damn slow this morning?" he says, chortling and annoyed.

I'm desperate here, hating my brother as much as I have ever hated him, gliding in my panic, skimming over the surface of self-hatred and fear and the what-about-me neediness that I struggle with on an hourly basis. We're waiting in a tiny room at the Stanford Radiation Department and I am obsessing about number one, not thinking about Carl, just wishing I could be with Casey, anywhere, out of here. And it is six a.m.

Carl starts to pray. Oh brother, here we go. He's trying to put himself in a peaceful place. There's a sign over his head: PLEASE DO NOT DISCLOSE PATIENT INFORMATION IN PUBLIC AREAS. And a poster of Charlie Chaplin winking in his derby hat. The sly smile of Chaplin in the radiation department.

Soon one of the doctors comes in. Carl is suddenly all tense again. "I have a few questions," he says.

He gets up and swings his arm. "I have to go fly casting next month in Alaska. I'm worried about the pressure of my T-6 and T-7 on the lumbar spine." The doctor who introduces himself as Dave, all so very California, begins to talk about rotations and his time fly casting. The two men are suddenly practicing their spins, shooting their arms, laughing about the big fish, moving themselves into an entirely different space. This is an entire world that Carl lives in that is away from me, and I watch with admiration for his mastery of the subject. Later, I write about this moment in my diary.

"He is an isolate like our father." My first instinct was to write his father. His. But standing in my room at the Garden Court, I realize I am standing exactly as my brother does.

He's in the room with the robot working on his spine for hours, all the while listening to *Parsifal*. He's thought of everything, the music, the DVDs.

The procedure works perfectly and we are able to have a festive lunch to celebrate. Carl eats two plates of hummus and three pitas. Later that day, I see Carl's doctor John Adler in the parking garage. I'm by myself. Adler pats my arm. "How is he doing?"

"Panicky," I say. "Angry. Okay."

It's hard for me to say even this much, I am so afraid of giving it any reality. I have the Brad syndrome—if I talk about what's real, it will happen. I am really struggling here with how misguided I am, how off my reactions are to Carl. I am pushing away all feelings, locked behind some herculean wall.

I hope you can talk to him about death, he says. Your brother is so type A. He thinks he can just bully this thing; he can will his survival. Eventually, the dam is going to break.

Adler has red hair and an open smile. He's worried that the procedure is going to paralyze him, I say. He's focused on that. He's terrified.

He's a very strong guy, Adler says. The doctors cannot believe he has this level of cancer. They have never seen anything like it.

When I get back to the hotel, Carl is out on the street, waiting to move his car. What are you doing, I ask?

I move meters three times a day, he says. Why waste fourteen dollars in the parking garage?

We're driving down toward the Stanford Medical Center and Palm Drive. The hospital complex looms ahead of us. Carl is driving, the oxygen tank on the floor. He's using the tubes but more out of nervousness at what awaits him today. The nurse at the desk tells him he needs a brain scan. Three hours of MRIs. I've just had one, he tells her. I've brought it with me.

What did it say? I ask.

He pulls me into a corner and tells me, Don't talk so loud. Someone will hear.

What did it say? I ask again.

It says I have twelve new lesions.

Twelve is, in fact, at least twenty.

On the brain.

The brain is the endgame, every cancer patient knows. It takes time, sometimes years, but it is the end.

There is nothing anyone can say.

Except this: This is not a catastrophe, I tell him. You can live for years with a lot of cancer in the brain. I am lying here. I can't help myself. He knows it and so do I. It is the very definition of catastrophe. I have an automatic response, believing my task is to make it better. Carl is right. I am a phony. No *bella figura* can make that go away.

I am overcome with nausea. The end of my brother's life, irrevocable, unchangeable. Soon, all of it will just fade, the moments of fusspot Elmer Fudd, the thrashing in the lake.

Dr. Adler is late this morning, and Carl is in a rage. He's not good at being powerless, either.

Carl sits with a nurse. I wait outside, and he believes I am in the waiting room.

This is what he says: They tell me when the end comes, if you're in good shape, that it is fast. Is that true?

Yes, she says.

That's good, he says. I am in very good shape. I did twenty pull-ups yesterday. That's how I broke my stitches.

And with that, I hear him laugh, a deep laugh that follows me down the hall.

This is what also happens in the world of the unwell.

San Francisco, a few days before.

He's waiting at the medical center, which is where the GVAX trial is. To qualify he has to have a lymph gland snipped out, and already he's furious because he's been up since dawn and at the hospital since six a.m. He's pissy with the residents. It feels like he's working himself up into a scene.

Uh-oh.

No sign of the doctors until nine a.m.

What does this tell you about the quality of care? he says.

He puts his glasses in a Baggie. Hold on to these.

I put them in my purse, too quickly for his taste.

Don't bruise my fruit.

I'll hold on to them, he says. They'll get scratched in there.

This is who he is.

He's being wheeled into the OR and he is saying in his lawyer's voice, loud and booming in the hall, No one is giving me any anesthesia, not one drop of Versed, I don't care how fast-acting, short-acting, until Dr. Jablons comes in. I will not agree to anything, sign a single paper, until I talk to Dr. Jablons. Am I making myself clear??

There's a flurry of "There's traffic on the highway. . . . Dr. Jablons is on his way," the blah-blah of trying to soothe another powerless patient. Finally, Dr. Jablons comes in, out of breath, filled with apologies, mumbling something about his kids and their illnesses and the traffic, and Carl is as impenetrable as ebony. "What time did you get up?" Meaning to San Francisco.

Four-thirty a.m., Carl hisses. What time did you get up? And on his face, the expression is that contemptuous dismissal, the defenses in full-out you-won't-kill-me mode, you son of a bitch. It's rude and insufferable, and I love him so much at this moment for being able to say it and not just wuss around because he's a fancy-shmancy big-deal doctor. I could scream.

They stare at each other. "I'm really sorry to have inconvenienced you," Jablons finally says. "It was wrong of me."

53

To cheer me up, my friends Peggy and Jim take me to hear Madonna at Madison Square Garden. I feel a titanic Carl rage coming on. We've come back from Stanford and I have had a phone call from Leonard Stern, real estate mogul of New York. I interviewed Leonard years ago about Donald Trump. He told me about rescuing Trump's business partner and close friend Louise Sunshine when Trump was pulling one of his fast ones. Stern sent her a check for $1 million to keep her share in a Trump building.

May I use this off the record? I asked him.

You can use it on the record, he said.

We have become friends and I have relied on Leonard's cunning wisdom to help me with Carl. He has seen Sam Waksal, the head of ImClone, at a wedding. Waksal is all sharp angles, working rooms of the powerful with a ratlike speed. Each Christmas he fills his TriBeCa loft with an A-list of New York's powerful. Waksal's wonder drug, C225—later called Erbitux—has been in the press as a possible cure for cancer. He styles himself an arbiter of taste and commerce, a sound-bite sharpie.

Stern has left the wedding, in his tuxedo, gone to his office in the middle of the night, and gotten my brother's medical reports. That is the definition of a friend.

At the wedding, Waksal looks at the reports and says, "I can cure Carl Brenner."

Call him, Leonard says.

I do, and Waksal doesn't return the call. Or another. I call him all week, and it becomes clear he is avoiding me.

This is understandable. Waksal is being bombarded with requests from dying patients.

I am not good at powerless. I am doing perky and it is not working. Nor for that matter is another quality I have, a relentless urgency.

I sense that something is going wrong with Waksal. It's just a vibe I have, but the atmosphere around him and ImClone reminds me of the aura surrounding the Brown & Williamson tobacco company when it was about to be exposed that it had been allegedly adding a compound found in rat poison to its cigarettes. There is darkness here.

We are sitting high in the tower of the Garden thirty minutes before the concert. Around us are kids in lace gloves and pink Material Girl T-shirts.

"Is this like a foe you are taking on that you think you can personally slay?" Peggy asks me.

It is clear now that Carl is trying desperately to turn the clock back. He spends weeks in New York around our kitchen table, the babble of family, Casey banging in and out with her new boyfriend from college. The part of him that kept me away has vanished. I finally have a brother, and soon I am going to lose him.

Leonard is furious that Waksal is ignoring my calls. He calls Waksal again. "Leonard, I have already helped one of your friends. You have played out your chits with me."

This is what you hear in the world of the unwell.

You have played out your chits with me.

All of this comes at me while I sit in Madison Square Garden watching Madonna writhing on the stage. I dislike her steely lack of humanity, the coldness that is under the performer's sexual pyrotechnics. I leave the concert and come into the steamy August night, low.

The next morning I am set to meet with Waksal's daughter Elana, who is running for City Council. I'm shameless now. I'm using every chip I can play to try to get this drug for Carl.

Pharmaceutical companies torture families over the subject of compassionate use. By eight a.m. I'm in SoHo, at the restaurant Balthazar, to have breakfast with the petite Elana. Casey's with me. My daughter has agreed to volunteer to help Elana Waksal with her campaign as a way to lure the 225 from Waksal's father. Elana preens at the table. It's clear I am going to get nowhere with her. "They are at the end of phase three," she tells us. "It is my uncle Harlan who makes all the decisions. Did you know that our grandmother survived Auschwitz? My father said that he would have come up with the cure for cancer to get his mother's attention. Well, he did."

She pauses and takes in the chic New York clamor of the downtown brasserie. "I am so proud of him."

One year later, Waksal is indicted on thirteen counts, including perjury, obstruction of justice, and securities and bank fraud. He currently is in prison until 2010.

The FDA eventually approved Erbitux to shrink tumors in colon and head-and-neck cancer patients.

I've met a gifted young cancer researcher who worked on a team at the National Institutes of Health. His name is Howard Kaufman and his expertise is vaccine therapy, an alternative way of treating cancer without the side effects of chemotherapy. We met at a lunch and it is obvious how involved Kaufman is with his patients. He is at Montefiore Medical Center, near the New York Botanical Garden and Morris Park. Talking to him, my eyes fill with tears. "I can't get my brother 225," I say. Kaufman says, "Come see me, let me see if there is anything I can do."

Now I am in his office and he is quietly seething. "There are hundreds of cancer drugs being researched and tested at the moment and there is only 2 percent getting to the patients. . . . Vaccines do not depend on chemotherapy, so the chemotherapy manufacturers do not want us to test our vaccines without using chemo as a booster agent."

It's in the early days of Kaufman's mission—to be able to push the FDA to allow them to give drugs being tested to patients whose cancer has metastasized. Some hospitals are better at this than others, Dana-Farber in Boston, for example. But most hospital internal review boards fear lawsuits if there are complications.

The early promising results with mice in the lab can lead scientists to jump, form biotech companies, announce results to hype a stock. There will be front-page stories and covers of *Time*. The example that is most often cited is the explosion of hope in endostatin, the wonder drug of world-class scientist Judah Folkman that did not live up to its initial test results.

You learn quickly in the world of the unwell not to leap at these miracle announcements, which zoom onto biotech fortunes after they're announced too soon in *The New York Times*.

From: Apple Man / Alamo@applecountry.com
Here on the farm, things are moving along. The pears are in bloom and the apples are showing pink. We have had a stretch of cooler weather that has drawn out the bloom more than we would

have liked. The bees are not too excited to get working when it is
below 60. Our highs have been in the low 60's, so we are getting
some bee activity but not enough. We are going to try to put on
some pollen by helicopter to help improve the set. The bloom
looks good for this year's crop.

All the best,
Marc

"She can be a little extreme," Carl says. "I want to warn you." We
are on the way to see a woman named Martha Hill. She's a fundamentalist who lives in a shady suburb and gives Bible classes to
the San Antonio society girls. "You may think she is a nutcase,
but she's done me a lot of good," he says, scowling.

We drive up San Pedro, passing the first suburban Solo Serve.
Neither of us says anything. For years this same street occupied
much of our conversation. It was country then, and our father
worried about expanding a faltering family business, pushing into
what seemed to be the underbrush, far from town. There were
worried nights and phone calls made from behind closed doors.

We pull up past a low brick suburban house. "She can take a
long time to answer," Carl says. A tall woman with a mane of
tweed hair and a blue velour robe suddenly fills the doorway.
Hanging from her neck is a large cross crusted with diamonds.
"Honeys, I am almost ninety and not so fast on my feet anymore,"
she says as she opens the door to her house. In the living room is
a grand piano with a collection of silver frames of famous minis-
ters, most noticeably the redheaded Reverend Billy Graham, the
man of piety who occasionally let slip with cracks about the Jews.

In her hand is a blue pamphlet. *The Greatest Need of Our Na-*
tion Today Is a Rebuilding of the Moral Fabric.

She can be a little extreme sometimes. But I have gotten a lot out of this.

"The Lord wants you," she says, pointing her finger at me. "Come to the Lord." Carl sits stiffly on a chair. Soon, he is down on the floor, right by the grand piano. "Lord, save Carl Brenner," she says. She begins to pray and read from the parables.

I sit on the sofa, feeling as if I have trespassed into some forbidden scene. Why did he want me to see this? What was he trying to say?

"You need to come to Jesus," Martha says suddenly.

"I'm Jewish," I say.

"That doesn't matter," Martha says. "Christ has your brother now, he wants you too."

"This is Heather's fault," I say when I get back into the car. "You always wanted to be accepted by those blond debutantes. Now they are reading the New Testament and you think you are in the cool club. What are you going to do? Join the Hare Krishnas next?"

"You don't know what you are talking about," Carl says. "Jesus' teachings have helped me a lot. You should read Matthew."

"Oh brother," I say. "You sound like you are in an episode of *Everybody Loves Raymond*. Next I am going to find you shaking a tambourine in front of Central Market."

"Shut up," Carl says. "You don't know anything about this, and it is none of your goddamn business."

"I am glad Mother is not alive to see this. She would make your life a living hell. You know exactly what she would say: 'Aunteen is trying to cash in while she can.'"

"Mother was crazy," he says. "They had a horrible marriage."

"They had the marriage they wanted," I say. "Daddy did not even come to New York to be with her except twice, the summer she had cancer and lived with me. And, for that matter, neither did you. What would Jesus say about that?"

Carl is now silent. My bomb has landed on the target. Silence was scary in our family.

We are back on San Pedro when Carl looks over to the left lane. "Look at that," he says. "There goes Aunteen."

We watch as she passes us in a Cadillac convertible, still in her bathrobe, gray hair flying.

"She's still driving? At ninety?" I say.

"Looks that way," Carl says.

"Jesus Christ."

Ilene and Carl are talking about the parable of the Woman at the Well when I find them at the Tokyo Inn, working through the sushi special deluxe. Carl grimaces, looks annoyed that I have arrived. I stay quiet while Carl bombs Ilene with questions about the New Testament.

"Do you know that parable?" Ilene asks me.

"Are you kidding?" I say.

Ilene laughs. "No reason that you should."

Carl gets up from the table and walks outside to make a call.

"You have to do something about this crazy fundamentalist."

"I wish I could," Ilene says. "She's told him that Jesus will heal him if he believes. He needs to believe this. It gives him hope."

"He cannot believe this," I say. "He was a trial lawyer. He sold juries with this kind of thing."

"He is scared to death," she says. "He'll believe anything now. I cannot take that away. I can only tell him what I always say: Sometimes healing involves something besides the physical. That is as far as I can go."

Now our Sundays are always with Ilene at the church. Carl wears a bow tie and lines up for communion with Eric and Bill, two gay colonels from the base. Carl recites the Nicene Creed:

> I believe in one God, the Father Almighty, Maker of heaven and earth, and of all things visible and invisible.
>
> And in one Lord Jesus Christ, the only-begotten Son of God, begotten of the Father before all worlds; God of God, Light of Light, very God of very God; begotten, not made, being of one substance with the Father, by whom all things were made.

In church, I hold his hand. *Ilene is good today,* he whispers. We watch her, and later remark on her striking resemblance. The same Eurasian eyes and cheekbones, but a tiny frame. She wears the white robes of a minister and stands in front of a large cross. Bright tapestry banners made by one of the churchwomen flutter over her head.

I write in my notebook:

> All postures come to this
> What You Want to Cultivate
> Engagement and Energy

In San Antonio, I take long walks beside the San Antonio River with my friend Naomi. She and her husband, Michael, are close to Carl, close to me. Carl often visits them in their frame house in the King William District. On Naomi's block, a few hundred yards from the San Antonio River, it is possible to close your eyes and believe you are in Mexico. From the river come the faint sounds of boom boxes playing mariachi music or laments from the singer Paquita. "What do you think he's feeling?" Naomi suddenly asks. "What does he say about it?"

"He's scared," I say. "He's angry all the time."

"But this Christian thing? He was worried how you would react."

"Why?" I ask surprised.

"Believe it or not, he deeply cares what you think about everything," she says.

"Really?"

Another Carl, closer to the end. It is Saturday in a Texas March. The bluebonnets cover the slopes of the hill country. I have come to bid my brother Carl a quick good-bye. I am on my way home to New York to attend to deadlines and fact-checking, last-minute edits on a complex piece of reporting. I find him in his office, sitting at a desk chair, wheeling back and forth. Hefty bags and a shredder are in front of him, and by the desk is an assistant he has hired that very week. The desk, which had once belonged to our father and grandfather, sits in a room that has a wall of portraits.

I overhear him: "William Trevor, Stephen Ambrose. Martin Cruz Smith, *Gorky Park*. *The Assassin's Cloak*, Carl Hiaasen, *Kick Ass*; *Harry S. Truman* by Margaret Truman."

"What are you doing?" I ask.

"What does it look like?" he says.

Near him are stacks of books. "I am listing all the titles," he says.

The reason?

For days, he has been staying up late at night, speaking into a tape recorder, listing every book he owns.

"How can anyone live with all of this?" my brother asks. He is suddenly choked by his possessions—the porcelain plates and books and Baggies and engravings and fruit posters and quilts. The etched glass and the linen napkins that did not leave with his divorce. "I am getting rid of everything," he says. He has invited a platoon of cousins and friends to cart away the fishing tackle, guns, and prints.

He is possessed by his mission—to erase every detail of his life. He will see to it that there is almost nothing left. No files of flirtatious letters from ex-girlfriends or diaries or e-mails that have the slightest degree of intimacy. He will, he decides, simply try to vanish without a trace.

There is a purpose in it. That he will make clear in a letter left for me on an empty shelf. There will be nothing a writer can draw on except memory, no letters, no sense of the man other than direct experience. He is in a joyous mood all day. He makes a date to meet a friend for soft chicken tacos at La Fonda on Main Avenue, knowing, but never saying, that he will drive his computer hard drive to a garbage dump on the other side of town. He fills the car with every piece of paper that could tell anyone anything about him. And for emphasis, he spends several hours erasing from his calendar all of his last dates, whom he saw and where. I will see my name, erased and faded, in day after day of entries. Marie to lunch. Dinner at Marie's. Marie over. Houston with Marie. China with Marie and Ernie and Allegra, Theater Girl. Palo Alto, Marie. Wenatchee, Marie. All of it erased, a blur. All of it carefully planned out.

He is often in his leather chair, set up in the room that is a shrine to the grandfather he never knew.

The voices float over him. He is flying high, over the orchards, the trees in front of him. A happiness is there, a sense of possibility. He imagines his grandfather stepping into an arcade to see Buffalo Bill. He knew he listened to Caruso. He knew he bought for his father a how-to book: *Instantaneous Personal Magnetism.*

I park in his driveway one day after dark. I hear music coming from Carl's house.

Somewhere there's music . . . how high the moon.

In the window, I see Carl dancing with Heather, his oxygen tank on the floor. They are lacquered to each other, the lights on very low. Stay happy as long as you can, Aunt Dorothy wrote to both of us soon after we were each engaged.

La Bella Figura.

The secret of everything.

Sinatra sings:

> Blue moon
> You saw me standing alone
> Without a dream in my heart
> Without a love of my own

He thinks about the women, moments in Jacuzzis, snapping towels at beaches, great meals, wines he has had.

Life.

Heart-drenching moments of happiness, feelings that he could fly forever through his orchards, trying for the first time the Honeycrisp.

Everything that happens next now seems completely understandable.

The pistol in the vault. Post-it notes everywhere: *Turn off the air conditioning. Gail has been paid.* The shelves meticulous.

54

Carl is with me in the car. We're driving through the barrio on the way to Delicious Tamales on Culebra Road to fill the car with chicken and bean Tex-Mex specialities. It's warm out, and we will find our way to a café by the San Antonio River. Casey is set to arrive today with her boyfriend Ariel. Spring break in the Texas hill country. All week we have been planning a party, an elaborate *merienda* with Mexican food booths and guitarists parked in the garden. Later, on his way with me to the airport, Carl is excited. Ariel, finishing film school, is laboring on a documentary that involves a shooter and a pistol.

"I'm taking them to the gun club," Carl says in the car.

I am half listening, zoning out in the way I do, nodding my head as if I am absorbing what he's saying.

"You're not listening. Goddamn it!" he says.

"You're taking the name of the Lord in vain," I say.

"I want Casey to know how to shoot a goddamn gun. A pistol protects you. I'll teach them both how to shoot. You need to know how to do that in life. Especially in New York."

"What are you talking about?" I say suddenly. "You think she is packing heat at Brown? Are you out of your mind?"

"If the Jews had been able to have guns, if they had known how to fight off the Gestapo, there would not have been a Holocaust," he says, scowling.

The party is on a Friday, and Carl is surrounded by dozens of friends. He eats two plates of Mexican food, stands up and walks around the tables, then quietly sits down on a sofa, breathing from his oxygen tank. "I don't want to live this way," he tells a cousin, a young surgeon. "Can you give me something when I get further along? I don't want to die of cancer. I will not die that way."

"You know I can't give you anything but morphine," our cousin tells him. "It's against the law."

"Who writes these laws?" Carl says, angry.

The next day he's taken the pistol out of the vault. We are out on the patio of his house, having take-out food from the French restaurant down the street. Lemon soufflés congeal in the sun.

"I'm serious about this," he tells Casey. "Just because you are a New Yorker doesn't mean you have to believe all that lefty stuff."

A silence.

"Look," he says, as if he has been rehearsing. "Any day you wake up and you do not get told 'Get your affairs in order' is a great day. All I want is for someone to say, 'Hey, we got this wrong.'"

I stay quiet, waiting for what is coming. Casey looks at me.

"Please do not go back to New York," he says to me. He is crying again. Casey looks away.

"I have to," I say. "Just for a few days."

"I just want my life back, the way it was."

You may wonder at what point we finally realized there was something vast and unknowable that connected us. Some larger truth, an understanding of what our time together had been about. It was a quiet Saturday, not that far from the end. Carl was sitting at his desk as usual when I came into his house. He was looking at a diary he had kept of a hunting trip to Brazil in 1975. At my suggestion, he had typed up a long account of a search for a jaguar in the jungle and sent it to *True* magazine.

"'Because of the piranhas, we never put our hands or feet in the water, much less swam, for more than an instance at a time,'" I read out loud. "'Instance?' What were you trying to say here?" Carl blushed. I flipped through twenty-five pages of sodden prose and read the final paragraph: "'I ate the heart of the jaguar in camp for supper as the Mayan Indians used to do in Mexico in 800 A.D. The jaguar had almost outlasted us, but our determination kept us going to a successful finish.' God, that is awful."

"I guess I wasn't meant to be Hemingway," he said. Then, suddenly: "What do you think happened?"

"They didn't like it."

"No, not that. With us. With the family."

"I don't know," I said. "Letters don't prove anything. They're a crutch."

He was suddenly looking at me hard. "Do you remember that one day we were at Uncle Henry's ranch and we were all fishing and I carried you on my shoulders. You were so little, you weighed nothing."

"You carried me on your shoulders?"

"I think I did."

"They started all that fighting, and then we never saw any of them again."

"You know, I never told you something. . . . I am sorry I was a terrible brother."

He started to cry. "I am afraid," he said.

"I know," I said.

"I was a terrible brother," he said again.

"It's not your fault," I said.

"Go forward," he said. "Just go forward."

Suddenly he was out of his chair, pulling his oxygen tank. "Stop letting the past occupy you. Your life is passing by."

A few days later, he writes out a detailed memo for Ernie and his accountant and leaves it on the shelf.

And of course a letter:

Dear Marie,
You will find everything you need on these shelves.
*   Go forward.*
*   Everyone limits themselves.*
*   Please forgive me for taking my own life. I don't want to*
burden you any longer. I hope you understand. I will miss you.
We will be reunited some day in Heaven, I pray and hope.
*   Please turn off the air conditioning.*
*   I send you my love, now and forever.*

*   Carl*

His shelves were completely bare.

55

Carl tells his girlfriend, Frika, not to forget the cilantro at Central Market. They're cooking dinner at home. Calls her on her cell phone. Uses the word "darling."

Then he calls me, sounding as he always does.

Annoyed.

Where have you been? he asks.

I do not tell him the truth. I do not tell him that I have been at the Met with Casey looking at the drawings of Leonardo da Vinci, the blurred lines of babies and mothers in umber tones.

Sfumato.

I do not tell him that what I am feeling is lightness, joy to be with Casey, a sense of momentary escape from illness, the ability to breathe.

I am waiting for Wayne, I say, mentioning my editor Wayne Lawson, whom he knows well. Wayne has been with me since I started at *Vanity Fair*, has shared the sound waves of every aspect of my life, pushing me to report the tough stories, to make the text cleaner, better.

He's a scholarship kid from Wisconsin who made his way to

Princeton by scoring the highest marks on the state Regents Exam. He dresses himself in ebullience, mentors the office interns, attends their weddings, takes them to their first performances at the Met or the New York City Ballet, regaling them with stories of great performers and their pratfalls, the moment that Nicol Williamson lost it in *Hamlet*, that kind of thing. He is Frank Crowninshield, frozen in time in his tweed jacket, quaffing martinis at the opera, frequently at our Thanksgiving and Christmas tables.

For Casey, Uncle Wayne.

We have a work ritual. Text on the table. Red pencils. Diet Cokes.

"Tell Wayne hi," he says.

"What are you doing?" I ask.

Gruff now. "I am looking at the tree plans. Trying to figure out the crop loads for Chelan. I've just about decided to put in ten thousand Honeycrisps in Pateros. It's risky, but if I am going to plant all those Honeycrisps, we have to do it now."

A pause.

"I love you," he says.

"I love you too," I say.

And again, "Tell Wayne hi. Don't forget," he says, annoyed.

Frika finds him moments later, facedown in a pool of blood on his lawn, a three-inch hole torn through his head.

I look up to see Ernie in the kitchen.

"What are you doing home?" I ask. "I thought you were at the office."

"Carl," he says. He cannot bring himself to speak.

"What about him?" I say. "I just spoke with him." Wayne and I are at the kitchen table, text in front of us.

A quiet Sunday. Red pencils. White pages on the wood. It's a long piece with a complicated narrative: France, Jews, shifts in scene. Wayne has walked in with an ominous announcement:

"Graydon will only give us thirteen thousand words; that means we have to cut six thousand words."

"It cannot be done," I say, furious.

"We have to," he says. "Or it will not run."

My life as a reporter there: trying to fit a book-length story into a magazine format.

I make a joke. "I'll kill myself."

Then, *Carl*.

He's gone.

"Gone where?" I say. "I just spoke to him. Frika is making dinner. He sounded okay."

I suddenly notice that tears are running down Ernie's face.

"Why are you crying?" I say.

"Carl is dead," he says. "They found him in the garden. The police are there."

"I just spoke to him," I say. Then, more furious, "This is so like him!"

"Darling, you are in shock," Wayne said.

No one tells you the truth, he said.

And in the end, he didn't, either.

Where do you get your bravery? I asked him. Had he made the decision then?

I've spent a long time trying to understand Carl's decision to put a pistol to his head. I've gone over his last hours again and again. I blame myself. Why did I leave?

I have no reasonable answer for that question.

Soon after I said good-bye, Carl went to Central Market to meet our friend Michael for lunch. Carl was trying to tell him something—what a special friend he had been, Michael later said. He was tense and Carl-like: words hummed around, but didn't really land. Then he jumped up and said he had to get to the post office before it closed. There he began to cough up blood.

I called Carl when I landed in the city. He and Frika were having a cozy dinner. "It is so romantic," Frika said. "We are making steaks. And apple pie." Then she whispered to me, "He's coughed up a bit of blood, but he's okay. He's terrified that he is going to be an invalid."

That night he stayed up, cleaning off his desk, *Parsifal* on full blast. A copy of the New Testament was by his side. And then the phone call to New York.

Tell Wayne hi. Don't forget.

They were, I realized now, the last words he ever said. Then he pushed himself out his back door, passing the wooden bowls of apples and the glass painting of a portly businessman that was on our father's office wall. There is a caption on the glass: *Sell and Repent.*

Carl was on his way to a place that only he understood, and for reasons that were his own. "I do not have long to live. No one should live this way," he said all that month, again and again. In the car, we passed a group playing basketball on a court. He was having trouble breathing. *I used to run that way, up and down the court: "Pass it to me, pass it to me," my arm in the air.*

We celebrated his life at Madison Square Presbyterian, and the choir sang the Kaddish, the traditional Jewish prayer for the dead. The church was packed, and done up to look like an apple orchard. Ilene stood on the pulpit with a cross behind her head.

I no longer think it is odd to call my aunt and hear her message on the church's answering machine: "Peace and love to you in the name of Our Lord Jesus Christ."

We made a vow to each other, Ilene said to a crowded church.

We were going to weave a new family, and no longer be part of the tapestry of brainy squabblers that had ended their time together in silence and separation.

Each year, there are two seasons in apple country that pull me across the continent to be at the farm. In May there is apple blossom time, when the Apple Queen rides down Wenatchee Avenue and a pink froth covers the Cascades. Marc always sends an early e-mail.

From: Alamo@applecountry.com
The Asian pears are starting to show some white so we know apple blossom time is actually coming. We are about ten days behind last year which is good.

And then harvest and the pace of the pickers working the rows at dawn. When Casey comes, we drive down from Seattle and look for the first break in the trees after Peshastin and the sign for the Big Y. There are vineyards all over now, and a Yahoo! data center opened in Wenatchee. If you go, try tasting at Tsillan Cellars, a destination sprawl of a villa. If you look to your left from the top of the hill, you'll see Carl's first orchard down the road from the Sunshine Fruit Market. Marc, now our partner, waits with Sadot in the truck. At the top of the Cashmere orchard, Sadot has erected a shrine hung with the Mexican religious medallions called *milagros*: a plaque for the Virgin of Guadalupe, patron saint of Mexico, and a Styrofoam cross with blue plastic flowers for Carl. There is an urn with some of his ashes too. The others are in the cemetery, near the remains of our parents and grandparents. None of this is the usual order of things, but what is ever usual in a family?

Sometimes you do not get to understand everything.

56

There is one day I keep thinking about. It wasn't a particularly big day, a holiday or anything like that.

It was, in fact, a small day.

I was in his home office with him in San Antonio. We were working on fruit orders. He was breathing with the small oxygen tank and I was typing on his laptop, answering the telephones, trying to figure out whether or not thousands of Asian pears had yet to arrive at Central Market in San Antonio.

I was sitting next to a bookshelf and I noticed it was covered with dust. There was dust on the books, dust over the wooden apples on the top, dust on the small bronze cuspidor that used to sit on our grandfather's desk. "Why isn't Sylvia cleaning this?" I asked. "It's horrible in here."

"Because I don't want her in my office," he said. "I don't want anyone in my papers."

"For God's sake," I said. "You are so damn paranoid. She took care of Daddy. You are a wack job."

In a minute, I was down on my hands and knees with damp

paper towels, lying on the floor, scrubbing down the dust kitties that were under his chairs, all over the bookcases.

"This is revolting," I said.

In his desk chair, Carl was laughing. "Hey," he said to George, on the telephone. "You should see my sister. Who knew her best talent was housecleaning."

And then, "Hey, Marie, let me ask you something."

"What?" I said, irritated by the mess.

"Do you do windows?"

We were both still laughing when Heather arrived a few minutes later. The three of us sat there all afternoon, eating Heather's just-out-of-the-oven oatmeal raisin cookies. We worked the phones and talked and tried to figure out how eight thousand Asian pears got lost somewhere in Idaho on their way from Washington State to San Antonio.

It was a completely nothing-special brother-sister kind of day.

An extraordinary day.

It could have always been like that.

If only.

But we had that. And, in the end, so much else.

Go forward, he said.

Okay, I would have liked to have been able to say.

And so much else.

ACKNOWLEDGMENTS

All books are collaborations. I am especially grateful to my editor, Sarah Crichton, and to my agent, Amanda Urban, who first inspired me to write about my brother and then encouraged me with exceptional wisdom and guidance. Thanks to Jane Stanton Hitchcock and Virginia Cannon, who suggested the title and subtitle. A special thank-you to Debra Helfand, Abby Kagan, Susan Goldfarb, Susan Mitchell, Cailey Hall, and Jessica Ferri at Farrar, Straus and Giroux for working under impossible deadlines.

I am grateful as well to Elise O'Shaughnessy, Elizabeth Mayo, Kerry Rubin, Sarah Smith, Ellen Hollander, Kathryn Belgiorno, Ann Arensberg, George Wood, Judy Barnes, Naomi Shihab and Michael Nye, Louis Michelson, and Lisa Chase.

To my cherished monthly lunch group: your support has made the writing of this memoir possible, as have the love and encouragement of so many friends.

I am grateful to my cousin Susannah Glusker, whose detailed biography, *Anita Brenner: A Mind of Her Own*, has filled in so many gaps in my understanding of her mother. A thank-you to my editors at *Vanity Fair*, Wayne Lawson and Graydon Carter, for their understanding of my need to take a swerve.

No one could have been more encouraging than my husband, Ernie Pomerantz, and my daughter, Casey Schwartz, and her brothers James and Adam. Casey and her father, Jonathan, advised, cajoled, and guided me with love and tenderness. My most profound gratitude is, of course, reserved for my brother Carl, whose courage, resilience, and discipline as he fought the battle for his life have shown me the way to be.

A NOTE ABOUT THE AUTHOR

Marie Brenner is writer-at-large for *Vanity Fair*. Her exposé of the tobacco industry, "The Man Who Knew Too Much," was the basis for the 1999 movie *The Insider*, which was nominated for seven Academy Awards, including Best Picture. She is also the author of *Great Dames: What I Learned from Older Women* (2000) and the bestselling *House of Dreams: The Bingham Family of Louisville* (1988).